NATURE LOVES COURAGE

By

Jacques Olivier
(Poloka Lele)

ICARO PUBLISHING

Icaro Publishing
Orcas Island, WA

© *2021 Jacques Olivier. All Rights Reserved,*

ISBN 13: 978-1-63848-767-8

Icaro Publishing, Orcas Island, WA

Book Jacket and Page Design: Matthew J. Pallamary / San Diego CA
Author's Photograph: Jacques Olivier — Orcas Island, WA

"While we are alive there is nothing in us which doesn't suffer change or modification. Everything is revelation, everything is a teaching, all is hidden treasure in things: each day the sun brings out sparks of originality. And everything is, within ourselves, as time goes by, the need for renovation, to acquire new force and light, to become aware of the bad not yet perceived, to enjoy the good not yet felt, to prepare, finally, our adaptation to conditions as yet unknown to experience."

Jose Enrique Rodo

TABLE OF CONTENTS

INTRODUCTION

"THE WORLD IS LIKE A RIDE IN AN AMUSEMENT PARK. And when you choose to go on it you think it is real. Because that's how powerful our minds are. It goes up and down and round and around with thrills and chills and its very bright in color and its very loud and its fun....for a while. Some people have been on the ride for a very long time and they begin to question "is this real or is this just a ride." And other people have remembered and they come back to us and they say" hey, don't worry don't be afraid ever because, this is just a ride.

We kill those people.

Shut him up, we have a lot invested in this ride. Shut him up. Look at my big furrows of worry. Look at my big bank account and my family. This has to be real. It's just a ride. But we always kill the good guys that tell us that, did you ever notice? And let the demons run amuck

It doesn't matter because it's just a ride. And we can change it anytime we want. It's only a choice. No effort, no work, no job, no savings of money. A choice right now between fear and love. The eyes of fear want you to put bigger locks on your doors and buy guns and close yourself off. The eyes of love instead see all of us as One. Here's what we can do to change the world right now to a better ride. Take all of that money we spend on weapons and defense each year and instead spend it feeding, clothing, educating the poor of the world which it would many times over, not one human being excluded and we can explore space together both inner and outer, forever in peace."

Bill Hicks

I began writing this book in September 2018 after moving to Orcas Island, part of the San Juan Islands in the Northwest corner of Washington state as a way to archive my life experiences. Inspired by Jim Channon (New Earth Army), a dear friend and mentor I met through Terence McKenna In 1999. Before I finished the first draft of this book I experienced a full cardiac arrest on September 13, 2019 during a Friday full harvest moon while performing David Byrne's song *"Lazy"* near the end of my musical set at Imagine festival on Orcas Island.

I literally died on stage with no pulse or heartbeat for over ten minutes, but good fortune combined with the heroic efforts of Angels on the scene, reanimated me with aggressive CPR and six electrical jolts with defibrillator paddles. The odds of surviving a "Widowmaker" heart attack like this are way under one percent, the odds of anyone reading this are less than that yet here you are reading the words of what should have been a dead man.

This event and the psychedelic experiences that prepared me for it have shown me there is no death, only a shift in consciousness to a different point of awareness unencumbered by a physical body consumed with maintenance and living in three dimensions. That learning never ends and there is no closure, only growth, change, and new experience.

There is a lesson to be learned in every moment and we determine the nature of the ride we are on based on our perceptions. Reality is Silly Putty not to be taken personally. Each of us shapes it to create the work of art that is our Life. Nothing is guaranteed except for change and transformation until our souls merge with the Oversoul when we shed our flesh encumbered bodies. Death is just the beginning of a shift in awareness. In my case it was another opportunity for rebirth and renewal.

I don't need to embellish this story and as fantastic as it sounds, I am profoundly grateful for the blessing of being here to finish telling the tale. While writing this, human experience on Earth is undergoing a transformation with profound consequences from a pandemic that restricts personal freedoms and changes how we live. All of this added an urgency to finish this project as I am acutely more aware of my limited time remaining incarnate in a temporary state of Grace, following an intimate conversation with Death.

Terence McKenna was open about his gratitude to his partner Christie for saving his life after a grand mal seizure in May 1999. During the last year of his life I witnessed a shift in his energy from his head to his heart, which was profoundly healing and beautiful. I now find myself in the same space that Terence was in at the end of the millennium in 1999 and have only love and forgiveness left in my Being. Psychedelics have prepared me for the ultimate transition when the Great Mystery is finally revealed.

I invite you to journey with me and share the musical adventure and dramatic comedy of my life to experience what it means to live by the words of Plato popularized by Terence McKenna.

" Nature Loves Courage".

Enjoy your fine selves and Aloha.

Image courtesy of Kat Harrison

SLINGSHOT TO HYPERSPACE

May 1998

Mateo was the first to go, but his first 2 attempts failed to produce results.

"Maybe you should try," he said. "I'm kind of a hard head. Let's try again. We can put more in this time. Remember what Terence said, 'Nature Loves Courage'."

We had purchased a gram of synthesized 5 Methoxy-dimethyltryptamine known as 5 MEO DMT from a lab in China when it was still legal in 1998 in the hopes of having an experience Terence McKenna had so eloquently described in his writings. Our synthetic crystal version matched the psychoactive component of Bufo Alvarus, a Sonoran River toad that bio-synthesizes Phylaris grass from its diet into 5MEO DMT to ward off attackers by stunning them.

Other sources of 5MEO DMT include the Adenanthera tree of the Argentine Atacama desert, Ayahuasca, and other plants. Hamilton Morris of **Hamilton's Pharmacopia** recommends using lab synthesized 5MEO DMT as opposed to 5MEO harvested from frogs for rituals as this natural source is becoming depleted.

I couldn't agree more.

After Mateo launched successfully from a third hit he handed me the pipe, laid down, and seemed to go into a deep sleep after exhaling the uniquely sweet smoke. It looked like nothing too exciting. I checked his breathing and heart and he appeared comfortable and relaxed.

About 15 minutes later he opened his eyes, grinning from ear to ear. "How was it?"

"WOW! Fucking insane! You have to do this!"

I felt reassured after witnessing this. After a few minutes of him attempting to describe the trip from the inside, I loaded the pipe.

With the distinctly sweet scent of 5MEO lingering in the air Mateo lit the flame and I kissed the bong containing ten milligrams of 5MEO, slowly filling my lungs with the entire dose. I held my breath and the sensation of falling upward into the sky overwhelmed me and I surrendered to the medicine. I entered into a brilliant white light all reference points obliterated and I no longer had a body. I existed as pure vibration in harmony with everything.

No me.

No time.

No space.

Only the sensation of eternal Presence that can only be described as Pure Loving Awareness or Supreme Consciousness; a glimpse of Infinity.

At some point I returned to my body and felt like I could reassemble myself cell by cell into a more perfect form reintegrating into the three dimensional world of normal waking reality.

This was the highest either of us had ever been, but I thought it did not quite match the experience Terence described in his books. With 5MEO there were no cartoonish visuals, machine elves, or deep colors. We rocketed past all that into an afterlife, or an approximation of the death state, the simultaneous experience of everything and nothingness at the same time in an alternate dimension of pure unadulterated, Absolute Awareness and Peace.

What follows is Mateo's perspective of this same event as told in his award winning memoir **Spirit Matters.**

"We examined the 5MEO white powder I had purchased by mail, smelled it, and tried to figure out the best way to calculate a dose, and smoke it. Sprinkling it over cannabis seemed like the most efficient method. Since I had purchased the 5MEO and initiated our meeting, we decided that I would try it first.

I approached my first hit with great respect and a healthy level of trepidation, evident by my sweaty palms and jittery stomach, but I tempered my fear with resolve. After breathing deep and centering myself, I took what I thought to be a healthy bong hit of 5MEO sprinkled over a small bed of cannabis, but I felt nothing more than a sense of heaviness.

"I don't know," I said to Jacques. "Maybe getting something like this legally through the mail is too good to be true."

"I heard sometimes it takes a second hit," he said, gently encouraging me.

I loaded up the bong with a little more and took a second hit. I felt more of the heaviness, but nothing more.

"This is bullshit," I said. "I think we got ripped off. I wasn't so sure about getting this stuff through the mail."

"Sometimes, I heard it takes a third hit," Jacques said, still not ready to give up.

I looked at him and weighed things through in my mind, then said, "Third hit, huh? Fuck it!"

I dumped a much bigger pile of 5MEO on top of the cannabis, took a solid third hit and instantly fuzzed out and dissolved the same way I had as a kid when I hyperventilated and passed out.

"Oh shit!" I thought as the terror came and annihilated me.

In those first moments of being swallowed and flooded by an infinite number of things, I felt my concept of the expansion and evolution of consciousness instantly confirmed before I dissolved into nothingness. I have no idea of how long I was gone. In my first glimmer of returning awareness, it came as a shock to me that I not only experienced annihilation of everything I knew by becoming both everything and nothing, but I survived it. In the midst of my receding awe and terror I knew I had received a gift of power that I had earned by putting myself on the line by my explorations, which amounted to asking questions. I experienced death again in response to this inquiry when I dissolved, embracing the ultimate thrill.

Over time I came to understand that the speed and power of 5MEO caught my ego off guard, and without its hold I was able to give up my "*self*" and merge with the Oneness and trust in perfection. Total surrender to a power greater than yourself is a sacrifice of *self;* a shift from selfishness to selflessness. Total surrender is also the essence of unconditional love. The more you let go and shut off your inner intellectual chatter, the more you receive. This is not only the key to 5MEO; it applies to visionary experience and the learning process in general.

Rationality is highly overrated.

Initially, I couldn't remember much about my experience, but I had the strangest feeling when I returned. Jacques plucked a string on his guitar, bringing me back to the here and now, only it didn't feel like returning to this reality, it felt turned around, as if reality had gone and now returned to me. He told me I had been moving around, talking and gesturing with my eyes open during my experience, but I had no memory of it. Once I felt grounded, we had a better idea of gauging an effective dose, so we prepared the bong for Jacques. I could sense the power and intensity of my own journey in the way Jacques readied himself with deep breathing, centering, and a blessing to himself. I also saw his fear and resolve when he took his hit.

He laid back and closed his eyes while I watched his breathing closely. His eyes jittered back and forth in a frantic r.e.m. state, then he sat straight up with his eyes bugged out of his head and let out one of the most terrifying screams I have ever heard; a truly primal one. Hoping the neighbors didn't hear, I went to his side and comforted him with words and gentle strokes until he fell silent. His scream was one of the eeriest things I have ever witnessed, reinforced by the look of pure terror in his widened eyes.

When I asked him about it afterward, he smiled and said that he could only remember bliss. I have no doubt that his mind blocked out the terror. It explained why I couldn't remember much of anything myself. I knew that Jacques screamed when the lid blew off of his subconscious, exposing all the fears and demons bottled up there.

In the days and weeks that followed, Jacques and I had many discussions where the two of us worked together to come to terms with what we had experienced. We both felt that our grasp of reality had been unhinged in a most exquisite way and we both felt disoriented, as though our former concept of ourselves had been bulldozed. In its place came new insights and conceptions of the nature of reality and our place within it.

Only one word can truly describe our experience.

Ineffable.

In our loss of self we experienced awe, ecstasy, and rapture, manifesting in an overwhelming flood of pleasure, love, and terror. The concept of a huge thrill only hints at its nature and intensity. Our physical boundaries fell away and we became the essence of our beings, literally swallowed up in creation by becoming one with it in pure awareness before returning once more to the physical. I can't articulate how good it felt to see Jacques on my return and how thankful I felt to have him there dancing on the edge with me. Our shared experience gave us an incredibly deep sense of brotherhood.

My ego death and rebirth sparked an ongoing cycle that continues to enlighten and expand me with a multitude of new and increasingly complex interconnected insights."

For another account, I refer you to Sasha Shulgin's description in **TIHKAL** with fifteen milligrams smoked under 5MEO DMT.

"At about 60 seconds after I smoked this freebase, I beheld every thought that was going on everywhere in the universe and all possible realities while I was wracked out with this horrible ruthless love. It scared the hell out of me. When I could see again (fifteen minutes later) it was almost as if there was an echo of a thought in my head saying I was given an extremely rare look at the true consciousness of it all. I've never been this hard since then. A definite ++++ out of 4 stars...off the charts!"
Sasha Shulgin

Poloka Lele   Alexander (Sasha) Shulgin   Drettie Page

ORIGIN STORY

I came into the world the only son to Georges Olivier and Monique Thibodeau on the 9th of August 1954 just after midnight in Montreal, Quebec Canada.

When my father was two, my grandfather Wilfred died of pneumonia in 1927 at the age of 29. My Grandfather had been a prominent attorney and rising star in the Montreal legal and political landscape. After he passed, Marguerite LaFontaine, my Grandmother sent my father George and his brother Jean to live on a farm outside of Montreal with their Grandparents Francois and Elizabeth Olivier, who raised them while she raised my aunt Suzanne alone in the city before remarrying. Marguerite's parents, my great grandfather who had been in the Canadian Parliament was Joseph LaFontaine and my great grandmother was Georgette Rochette.

Marguerite my grandmother was an elegant cultured woman who kept an immaculate home filled with fine furniture and appointments. She always maintained a dignified, cultured, pleasant, loving, kind demeanor.

Monique Thibodeau, one of 4 girls and one boy raised in a wealthy environment. Her father had been the successful owner of a shoe factory that went out of business in the depression. After losing his business my grandfather went to work and lost a thumb while operating heavy machinery to support his large family.

When my father was sixteen he and his brother moved to the city and with the help of his mother got a job working for the city as the mayor's assistant which kept him out of World War II with a deferment. My parents met at a ski resort after the war, marrying in the early fifties. My father later told me that they had lost their first child before having me.

In the fall of 1958 my parents moved to Los Angeles after visiting Paulette, one of my mother's sisters. After experiencing the beautiful Southern California weather which stood in stark contrast to the winters of the East coast we settled in Eagle Rock, a community in northeast Los Angeles where I attended eight years at St Dominic's Catholic grade school followed by Pater Noster all boys Catholic High School for another four years.

After buying a small two bedroom house in Eagle Rock in 1960 we became a part of the community I spoke only French-Canadian, but learned English in kindergarten and first grade while my parents retained thick Quebecois accents. My mother worked making me a latchkey kid in a relatively safe neighborhood.

Music has always been major source of enjoyment and comfort for me, especially in the 1964 when I was about 10 years old. My parents bought me a Silvertone acoustic guitar for $15 from Sears one Christmas and lessons with a woman in the neighborhood, but I soon quit due to the pain involved and the fact that the guitar was a toy and unplayable, even for an accomplished player. I wanted to play rock and roll and my parents wanted me to learn Flamenco and Classical music. This, coupled with my dislike for the teacher's personality and appearance made me switch my attention to sports and later to motocross racing.

We were one of the first families on the block to have a color television and a stereo system with two large separate speaker cabinets sitting six feet apart in the living room. My friend Fritz and I spent hours pretending we were playing in a band, switching off between tennis racket for guitar and pillows for drums while mimicking the Beach Boys or the Beatles and practicing our rock star moves.

I met my first girlfriend Sheri at age 19 when I attended and earned an Associate Degree at Glendale College. I was a small kid until I shot up to 6ft 2 inches in the summer of 1970 after going to Hawaii for the first time with my father. I remember the sweet scent of plumeria pervading the warm air when I got off the plane in Honolulu, and in that moment I recognized Hawaii as one of my true spiritual homes and vowed to live there one day.

"Being brave is a thing that one never regrets."
Ken Symington

Monique Olivier (Mom)

George Olivier (Dad)

Justin & Carmella Thibodeau

Marguerite Olivier (Grandmother)

FIRST AWAKENING

Sheri got me high on cannabis for the first time and deflowered me on New Years Eve in my surfer van just out of camera range at the 1974 Rose Parade in Pasadena. I was a late bloomer and still a virgin when I entered junior college as an un-cool nerdy nineteen year old. Life changed dramatically that night.

My first psychedelic experience came on December 24 1974 at the age of twenty one in my second year at Glendale Community College provided by Ken, a friend whom I had known since first grade. We had both suffered thru twelve years of Catholic school, boy scouts, and altar boys. Ken was ahead of me in mental and physical maturity since he had a girlfriend in high school he was having sex with. He had previously taken LSD and was eager for me to try it, but I was fearful having believed all the anti-drug propaganda of the late 60's. At first I resisted his cajoling but finally relented when he overcame my objections with the line, "How can you know anything about something without having experienced it?"

An hour after ingesting three hundred micrograms of orange sunshine in a tiny microdot I felt an electricity in my body as if some switch had been turned on allowing me to feel deeper with a heightened sense of expanded consciousness. Colors intensified and everything became *alive* and charged with an energy I had never been aware of before. Boundaries dissolved revealing creation in all its naked glory and extreme joy filled me, replacing the boring depressed state of my previous humdrum life. This was the miracle I had always dreamed about. My enthusiasm for psychedelics was born and has never gone away. I wanted the feeling to last forever.

Paradise truly is an inside job.

Weed, sex, and psychedelics had a profound impact on the rest of my life and triggered the beginning of my transformation as a human being, and I was hungry for more. There was something magical and otherworldly about the psychedelic experience, yet it was familiar.

For Ken it was another thing to party with. He drank beer to take the "edge" off, usually ending up more drunk than high, for me alcohol and acid were like oil and water that did not mix well. Psychedelics felt more like teacher spirits to be respected as the powerful tools they are rather than drugs to party with.

EARLY EXPERIMENTS

The next few years became a period of experimentation with a variety of substances. It was the 1970s and nothing was off limits. I tried psilocybin, peyote, San Pedro, and was fascinated with the use of plant medicines by indigenous cultures, confirming my intuition that they were considered sacraments used in divination and rites of passage. I also dabbled with more conventional pharmaceutical drugs like Cocaine, PCP, Angel Dust, and Quaaludes. My aversion to needles and lack of connection kept heroin off the list as well as speed, and other amphetamines which were unattractive due to the fact that I was normally high energy. The speed freaks I knew looked unhealthy.

Alcohol was unattractive as a result of my father's verbal and emotional abuse of my mother and I. When he was drinking he had a Jekyll and Hyde personality and became the life of the party with his friends while saving his dark side for his family. My interest in altered states grew as the sixties saw the culture explode with new ways to get high. Sex, Drugs, and Rock and Roll became the mantra for my generation of Baby Boomers.

In 1973 I experimented with Angel Dust known as PCP, an animal tranquilizer sprayed on mint leaf, making it possible to smoke. Ken and I bought joints from Teddy, a mustachioed rotund man who bred Himalayan cats and had access to large amounts of PCP. It was all fun and games for a couple of months in 1975 until Teddy's true motivations were revealed.

On Christmas Eve Teddy convinced Ken and I to hit a pipe of pure PCP with him, something far more concentrated than our mint leaf joints. We became incapacitated in the extreme within seconds and Teddy made his move to initiate a sexual encounter. We somehow managed to get away and I spent the next four hours puking and barely conscious, hanging out of my truck in front of a hospital. That experience ended my angel dust phase.

When Sheri transferred to Long Beach State in 1974 it marked the end of our sexual relationship, but she introduced me to Carlos, her new friend from Columbia, and he introduced me to cocaine. He had pounds of pure Peruvian abalone flake smuggled in thru Seal Beach Harbor. He fronted me ounces which I broke up and sold in grams to friends in the San Fernando Valley at a handsome profit. I had no shortage of buyers at one hundred dollars a gram. This went on for about six months but I was naïve and unaware of consequences both legal and otherwise of dealing cocaine. Twelve years of sheltered Catholic upbringing left me unprepared and at twenty years old I was not cut out for that kind of life.

Over time things degenerated and unravelled on both ends. Carlos was losing his shit from doing lines the size of drinking straws every ten minutes and he was becoming paranoid, with good reason. On the other end I began hating all of my clients and "friends" who showed up at my door at three in the morning teeth grinding, wanting more blow.

I stopped selling and snorting coke in 1977 after meeting Laura who became wife and mother to our only son Maximillian. Love came to my rescue for the first of many times in my life in the form of Eros, the Goddess of Love.

"The psyche has a thousand ways to terminate a life that has become meaningless".

Carl Jung

Laura with 1956 Ford F-100 Panel Truck

LOVE & TRUST

I met Laura, a gorgeous nineteen-year old Argentine Latina in 1976 and she became my first real love. I was twenty one and she was nineteen. After a week of intense flirting at work she cut in line ahead of me at the water cooler. "Excuse me." she quipped as she wedged herself between me and the water cooler.

"There's no excuse for you!" I said, parroting an old Groucho Marx line.

This began a lifelong relationship with many highs and lows. I was smitten with her and willing to do anything to be with her. She had been dating and sexually active since her early teens and I was less experienced than her and naïve in comparison.

I loved music, but could not yet play an instrument because of my initial experience and the fact that my Catholic college prep education had been full of math, science, english, religion, and history, but no art or music.

Although I was attracted to Laura physically, we seemed to speak different languages. I suggested taking LSD together and when she hesitated I asked, "Do you trust me?"
"Yes."

On a beautiful sunny day in January 1977 we each dropped two hundred and fifty micrograms of windowpane LSD together on a nude beach at Point Dume, California. Years of inhibition and programming melted away as we stripped off our clothes and basked in the Malibu sunshine while frolicking in the waves of the Pacific, feeling free and bonding deeper in the process.

I collected and read books on consciousness expansion by

Timothy Leary, Alan Watts, Aldous Huxley, Robert Anton Wilson and newer to the scene, Terence McKenna. I saw that drugs expressed their character through the humans that took them and the people who took those drugs reflected their effects through their own personalities. There is a lesson to be learned in every experience even if the lesson is to avoid that experience in the future. Many drugs have possessive spirits and involve shame, dishonesty, or secrecy around their use.

Psychedelic purists seemed funny, uniquely articulate, empathetic, irreverent, and intelligent, and I resonated with and was drawn to psychedelics, recognizing their extraordinary teaching potential. I was eager to learn more about myself and how to integrate them more intelligently into my life. Consciousness was and still is the only game in town and psychedelics hold the keys to the kingdom. Having been educated in highly structured Catholic schools, Irish Catholics held a particularly strong influence on me, resulting in Leary, McKenna, Shelley, Yeats, and Tom Robbins dominating my list of favorite writers.

Laura introduced me to Randy Rhoades, the legendary guitar player from Ozzy Osbourne's first band after Black Sabbath, the first concert I went to in 1971. Randy had been Laura's first boyfriend and lover in high school.

His first band Violet Fox, he played with Laura's brother Alberto in high school and later played in Quiet Riot before joining Ozzy's band. He was friendly and cordial and I sensed him sizing me up as a potential partner for Laura. He was a Rock Star and I was a psychedelic music fan who didn't play an instrument. I decided in that moment to quit accounting classes at CSUN and buy a new Yamaha acoustic guitar and learn how to play. I longed to be the man that Laura wanted so I started private guitar lessons because I thought it was the way to her heart. It never even occurred to me that she was attracted by the fact that I was *not* a Rock Star.

I later learned that Randy wanted Laura to accompany him on an Ozzy tour as his clothing designer. She would most likely have been on the plane that crashed and took Randy's life had she gone.

"Each friend represents a world in us, a world possibly not born until they arrive, and it is only by this meeting that a new world is born"

Anais Nin

ROAD TRIPPIN

I spent five years from 1978 to 1983 learning to play guitar and studying music theory while restoring my 1956 Ford F-100 panel truck that Laura and I travelled in through the United States in late 1979 after quitting our jobs as claims examiners at Blue Cross.

Our first escape from Los Angeles in 1979 would not be our last. We drove my fully restored panel truck from LA to Montreal along Historic Route 66, which I had traveled many times before with my parents. This time the trip would be on LSD with my future wife as we both tasted freedom for the first time while living our version of Timothy Leary's turn on, tune in, and drop out. At 23 and 21 we were young, wild, and full of dreams yet still very "green".

We visited my cousins in Montreal for the next month and moved on with no particular destination in mind. In Buffalo New York we connected with Janice and Jeff, new friends who owned a head-shop named Starseed Enterprise. I had written a letter to Janice after reading Tim Leary's book **What does Woman Want?** thinking that Starseed, mentioned in the book had some affiliation with Tim. It didn't, but we had made new friends.

One day after failing to reach my mother on the phone I learned that she was in the hospital after having a stroke. We drove back to LA arriving in California five days later. It was 1980 and John Lennon had just been shot. My mother was sick and the party was over, so we found ourselves back in Los Angeles, jobless, broke, and homeless ending the innocence of our early twenties and a time to reinvent ourselves in a major way.

"The danger of beauty in the very young is that it can make the business of life seem deceptively easy"
                    Julian Fellowes

" Nothing lasts but Change "
                    Spencer Eldridge

A NEW REALITY

With a reference from a high school friend I landed a job at the Fabulous Forum, the premier sports and entertainment venue in Los Angeles, home to the Los Angeles Lakers and Kings as well as host to most of the major concerts and events in LA.

Laura found a bookkeeping job at Capitol records and we moved into an apartment in West Hollywood near the Whisky a GoGo.

A new era had begun.

I soon became the lead of the Event crew responsible for supporting event operations including driving the Zamboni ice machine to resurface the ice between periods of Kings games, changing broken basketball nets during Lakers games, and other duties during major events.

I had full backstage access which made it a fun job where I gained valuable insights into the entertainment industry. I got to watch all the top musicians perform up close and I was learning to play guitar while making valuable business connections. I worked at the Forum from 1980-1986 during the Lakers championship era with Magic Johnson and Kareem Abdul-Jabbar when they won 3 world championships and I worked hundreds of concerts by all of the major artists including, but not limited to David Bowie, Led Zeppelin, Queen, Tom Petty, Van Halen, Yes, and every other big musical act from 1980-1986 at their peak.

Pink Floyd became my main influence musically and philosophically. They never played the Forum, but I saw the Dark Side/Wish You Were Here tour in 1973 at the LA Sports Arena on a hit of 4 way Windowpane acid.

Laura and I had a full meltdown at Anaheim Stadium for the Animals Tour in 1979. We had taken a hit of LSD and found ourselves surrounded by huge inflatable cartoonishly horrific pigs, sheep, evil schoolmasters and dogs while in the distance Pink Floyd were onstage playing the dark sounds of Animals seemingly mocking us in a cynical commentary about the state of our worlds and life in general. I felt the vibe and grabbed Laura's hand and headed for the exits to escape the madness of the moment. We spent the rest of the concert in my panel truck in the parking lot trying to sort out what happened. The question for me was "What are they *on*?, and the answer came to me that they were *on stage* which set them apart from the maddening crowds. This realization served as a huge motivator for me to get better and focus more on my instrument. This event became a major foreshadowing experience. I saw psychedelics as a camera that could take pictures of the future and bring them into the present as motivation to construct a new reality.

Energy follows attention.

We returned the following night and having gotten the message the first night did not feel the acid and watched calmly from the stands feeling disconnected from the concert.

Every event at the Forum was a spectacle that I became a supporting cast member in. I could write an entire book about those six years alone, but a few experiences stand out.

During half time at a Lakers playoff game I was getting a mop to clean up a spill near the Lakers locker room. When I attempted to enter the supply room where the mops were kept I felt resistance from behind the door. Stepping back, I kicked it open revealing three surprised men doing bumps of cocaine. Jack Nicholson from One flew over the Cuckoo's Nest, Lou Adler, a major record producer for the Mamas and Papas, and Elmer Valentine, the owner of Whisky a Go Go and Roxy. They had floor season VIP seats next to the Lakers bench and were in the habit of meeting in the supply room to get high during half time. I advised them of the pitfalls and agreed to meet them for future games in the employee lunchroom that I had a key to which became a regular ritual of smoking weed and doing bumps during halftime at Lakers games. It turned into a mini party with other celebrities and guests among them the actor Michael Douglas of Wall St fame, who was an investor at the LA Weekly where I ended up working after the Forum.

In 1984 during a half time party, I introduced Jack, Lou, and Elmer to the book **Life Extension** by Durk Pearson and Sandy Shaw which contained information about Diapid, a drug prescribed for controlling frequent night-time urination that contains the neurotransmitter vasopressin which is depleted with cocaine consumption and is responsible for the head rush that comes when someone ingests cocaine. Taking Diapid minimizes the crash effects by restoring Vasopressin to the brain.

One day Jack Nicholson was passing me a joint when the lunchroom door opened and my boss walked in. He looked around and saw me barking, "Get out of here!" which I promptly did. Surprisingly I didn't lose my job. That came 6 months later during the 1984 Olympic games.

I became bored during a poorly attended China versus Germany women's Olympic basketball event. Our crew had been issued bright orange and purple uniforms to wear during the Olympic events. When I went to the top of the empty nosebleed section to smoke a joint a patron saw me and the next day I found myself jobless.

"Existential worry is preposterous. We don't know enough about it to worry."   Terence McKenna

Jack Nicholson   Me   Lou Adler

Los Angeles Kings All Star Game with Zamboni crew

MEDIA MATTERS

In 1984 I was playing guitar in the **Mutts**, the first band I had joined after answering an ad for a guitarist in the LA Weekly. My mother crossed over on Memorial Day 1983, two months after joining the **Mutts**, I went to St Joseph's hospital in Burbank to visit and found her intubated and near death. She passed as I held her hand. I felt a charge of electricity shoot from my arm, through my body, and out the top of my head. It felt like hitting my funny bone at the elbow.

After her final breath I channeled my grief into the intensity of playing punk rock in the mid Eighties LA underground music scene. Fierce and passionate onstage I stayed physically and unpredictably spontaneous, ending up drenched in sweat every show, which made for a great show. People compared us to MC5, Iggy Pop's first band for our onstage intensity.

We played every club in LA including the Whisky a Go Go, the Roxy, Palace, Madame Wongs and Cathay de Grande. We gained momentum in the 80's LA music scene with music that was a cross between the Ramones and the Rolling Stones, a Ramoning Stones if you will, with strong left leaning political underpinnings from our singer's deeply held political beliefs. We wanted press coverage. My next job at the LA Weekly was perfect for that.

MTV Event playing with Adam Ant, Fishbone, and The Bangles Universal Ampitheater - 1986

1984 Mutts at the Whisky A Go Go

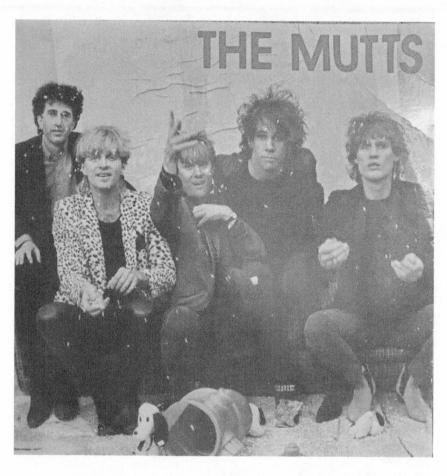

1984 EP

I started working as a driver at the Weekly in late 1985, the same year Terence McKenna was featured on the cover and interviewed by Jay Levin, founder and Editor of the wildly popular alternative LA paper. I first heard Terence on the late night radio program Roy of Hollywood in my car while driving home from my job at the Forum and was instantly drawn in. The things he said about psychedelics felt like my deep inner thoughts that I couldn't articulate, as if he was reading my mind.

I had seen Tim Leary on his stand-up philosophy tour debate with Richard Nixon henchman G.Gordon Liddy and attended a couple of events where Tim introduced Terence to the world. The LA Weekly article featuring Terence came out in 1985 marking a defining moment that boosted his career and profile. At the same time I was experiencing a surge in my musical and artistic development in the Mutts, my Weekly job helped raise the band's profile by providing press coverage from connections I made with writers and critics.

The next five years became an incredible ride on the rock and roll circus as the Mutts bigger and more high profile gigs came sharing bills with Fishbone, the GoGos, Red Hot Chili Peppers, the Bangles, Adam Ant, and many other well known bands. We released two independent records, got courted by major record labels and had a blast playing live and touring the West coast of the USA.

Laura and I met a man named Bill who owned the rights to the artist MC Escher's estate. He wanted to invest in a band, probably to launder drug money. After attending a July 4th LSD enhanced fireworks show that Bill sponsored in Watsonville California, Laura and I conceived our son Max in the afterglow of the display with explosions of our own passionate throes of Love.

Bill ended up backing a band called Camper Van Beethoven that signed to a major label. The major record companies preferred less political bands like Guns & Roses, Poison, and Motley Crue, over the Mutts who were an in your face post punk outfit with strong political opinions in the lyrics, like the Clash.

Looking back it's a good thing we didn't "make it big." We would have surely self-destructed given our penchant for partying and over-indulgence. As it was, we enjoyed all of the highs of the rock and roll life experience, building something and growing a band, while avoiding the inevitable fall from grace.

My early experiences with psychedelics taught me the value of direct experience over messages from the culture of "thing fetish" and conspicuous consumption, which put me out of step with many. I was always in love with the early stages of creation, addicted to the buzz of the initial phases of mastering things, and less concerned with marketing and monetization of art.

I was motivated to be a musician for self-expression and winning the love and approval of Laura my Muse, and less about the trappings of being a Rock Star, although I admit that I did desire some of those things. I also recognized the beauty of keeping things smaller, simpler, and personally rewarding over exploiting them for the sake of acquisition or control. Along with ownership comes the responsibility of protection and maintenance until things own *you* rather than you owning them. I placed value in living simply so others may simply live.

My friend Bruce Pavitt of Sub-Pop fame described these pitfalls in an NPR interview "This is how we built it" making the case for keeping things smaller and sustainable. Nirvana and Cobain are a perfect example of what can happen when massive commercial success and fame devour a sensitive artist. Everything happens exactly as it is meant to, and timing is *everything* in life.

"You can't always get what you want but sometimes you get what you need." Rolling Stones

"All you touch an all you see is all your life will ever be" Pink Floyd

"Thinking is the best way to travel" Moody Blues

HERE COMES THE SON

Max was born April 26th 1987, two days before Laura's thirtieth birthday. I was thirty-two and had been in the band for six years, but now preferred to stay home with my young family rather than playing in bars for drunks. In early 1988 I quit the Mutts and started a new project with Mutt singer and founder Spencer that we named the Painted Word. Spencer had been more supportive of me becoming a dad while the other 3 band members were not so sure. They went on as the Mutts and Spencer and I performed more relaxed music as the Painted Word which was named after the book by Tom Wolfe.

The transition from Rock guitarist to new father proved to be harder than I anticipated. I was accustomed to being the center of attention which Max now became, but once I understood that I became a better father and a better person. Being Max's father has been the single most powerfully transformative event of my life.

My job at the LA Weekly took more of my time, energy, and focus. By 1989 Hip Hop made its way to the scene, ultimately eclipsing all other music genres. Spencer moved to New York, the Painted Word ended and I focused on my job and family, soon becoming Production Supervisor at the LA Weekly. I bought a new house in Palmdale, 50 miles north of LA and commuted four days a week. The Rodney King riots of 1992 became a major factor in my decision to get out of LA. Meanwhile Terence McKenna's career had taken off making him a global star in the literary and the psychedelic rave scene.

The mid-nineties also saw my twenty-year marriage to Laura end due to a variety of reasons creating the perfect storm that neither of us could weather. Alcohol played a part in my denial and inability to transition to a more stable lifestyle. I had never been a heavy drinker, but occasional use affected my emotions negatively. My divorce was devastating. We had met at a young age and had difficulty with personal boundaries. Coincidentally, Terence's marriage hit the rocks around the same time with similar outcomes. It is hard to navigate divorce when children are involved, and Terence and I shared the hardships of emotional pain and trauma over failed marriages.

My divorce with Laura was final in late 1996 and in early 1997 I attended a workshop at the Esalen Retreat in Big Sur led by Terence McKenna, which fell on my birthday weekend in August. Esalen was where Laura and I were married in 1986 so I attended the Terence workshop as a birthday gift to myself to reconnect with my psychedelic roots and explore a deeper nature of self and of Being.

Terence was fond of saying "The best story wins," a philosophy I take to heart.

Grandma, Laura, and Max

New family, new car.

MEETING McKENNA

The yearly event at Esalen sold out and I was one of thirty attendees lucky enough to participate in an intimate weekend where Terence shared his latest ideas with a core audience. It also afforded me one on one time with him for the first time. We connected after the first night's talk, sharing mutual stories and feelings surrounding our broken families and fatherhood. We also shared a love for Hawaiian culture and psychedelics. Terence encouraged me to attend an Entheobotany Seminar for a week of immersion into the world of sacred plant medicines.

I went to my first one in Uxmal, Mexico in February of 1998, joining an ongoing series of yearly events with other speakers, among Sasha and Ann Shulgin, Paul Stamets, Jonathon Ott, Christian Ratche, Rob Montgomery, Giorgio Samorini, Michael Bock, Ralph Metzner, Marc Pesce and others with Terence being the Headliner; pun intended. Political tensions in Mexico moved the conference from Palenque to Uxmal in 1998, in a drier part of Mexico where there were no known sources of magic Cubensis mushrooms growing, making morning glory seeds the only psychedelic plant available. Palenque, where the conference returned to has a Cubensis flush every year at conference time.

We were shown how to make a cold-water Lysergic Acid LSA infusion with the Morning glory seeds and shown where they grew. Several of us explored this after the first evenings lecture while others went into town to purchase Ketamine, known as Special K, which was available over the counter in Mexico. I spent the first night at the hotel bar drinking tequila shots while feeling others out before breaking out whatever stashes people brought to the conference. Spot the Mole was a tradition at these events as it was assumed that they were being monitored by law enforcement agencies.

Salvia Divinora is a plant in the mint family that was the latest plant of interest and we were invited to volunteer as part of testing of Salvinora A, the purest distillation of the psychoactive ingredient in the plant. I applied for the study, but was low on the list due to my initial hesitation. Others who had smoked the Salvinora A had mixed results ranging from strangely and profoundly weird to terrifying.

I was fine with the fact that I missed out and I later learned that smoking Salvia was considered a desecration by indigenous Mexican shamans who took the plant orally by holding a bindle of leaf in their jaws, allowing the plant to mix with saliva for slow absorption. Smoking the pure extract proved too much for many and not particularly enjoyable. One man who was negatively affected lost his sense of self and reality for years following his experience.

On the final night in Uxmal a few of us bribed the guards at the Mayan ruins next to the conference hotel to let us stay past closing time. Someone broke out some LSD and we tripped all night, bathing in the powerful Mayan energies and time traveling through the centuries of beauty there. The lone sound of a digeridoo added to the sense of timelessness by punctuating the Sun's rise, signaling the end of our journey. Upon returning to the hotel I had one of many self induced ego deaths which reset me by transforming aspects of my personality, making room for a more accepting, loving version of me.

I needed to forgive myself and Laura and move on from the LA Weekly which had become my own custom made prison after fifteen years. I imagined headlines to the story: "X-Mutt and LA Weekly employee dies mysteriously in Mexico while attending a psychedelic conference," and all the negativity that would come with that scenario. I imagined my son without a father and other scandalous implications concerning the psychedelic group I was with.

As it turned out I didn't die, but had glimpsed a view of a world without me. It would go on, but this psychic death and rebirth of the ego gave me the courage and opportunity to change what needed to be changed without fear. It was time for me to be reborn creatively and "Put the Art pedal to the metal" as Terence would say, in response to a culture and a world in decay. Music was my passion and it returned to my life, defining me in my next incarnation under the name NatureLovesCourage. This pattern of ego death and rebirth became a running theme in my life, which has been filled with many self-induced reset events culminating in one unexpected near death experience, known as an (NDE).

Terence McKenna – "Follow the plants!"

The fullness of this moment
Hold on tightly, let go lightly
A full cup can take no more
The candle burns low
The razors edge
Nor this moment can be relived
So now
Hold on tightly
So now Let go lightly

Timothy Leary

ART AND INSPIRATION

Fellow Uxmal attendee Nick had recorded a live rap of Terence's at the conference, which I included as the seventh track in Catal Huyuk, the first album by *NatureLovesCourage* released in January 2000, and available at *NatureLovesCourage* on iTunes, Soundcloud, CD Baby, Facebook and other digital platforms. I did an independent CD release of 1000 CD's with a picture of Terence climbing the Mayan pyramid at Uxmal with Mateo sitting at the top as a CD cover. It was not until September of 2010 that my music switched to digital distribution making it available worldwide for the first time, thanks to one of the greatest loves of my life, Jacqueline.

That album, conceived at the end of the twentieth century post mushroom trip came complete with all the lyrics coming in a single download while I sat on the banks of a stream flowing next to Hotel Chan Ka in 1999 Chiapas.

I became a conduit that the words and music poured through   as if the words wrote themselves rather than anything I had created. I recorded it live in a rehearsal studio in LA with long time friends Laurence, Gary, and Cordell on a single take which we mixed and remixed with multiple layers of production added by Laurence S, Nick Doof, Loopy C, and myself.

Catal Huyuk by *NatureLovesCourage* marked my return to the world of music after 15 years and I was ready for the twenty-first Century. It received rave reviews from Terence, Tom Robbins, Sasha and Ann Shulgin, Bruce Pavitt of SubPop Records and Michael Simmons of the LA Weekly. Lorenzo Hagerty used the EL Alien track as an intro to his newly launched Psychedelic Salon podcast in 2000 where it remains so to this day.

Reviews

NatureLovesCourage are a reflection in the rain puddles of a vast and primal and ominous force, a bio-electricity that has never known bio-insulation"

Tom Robbins

"I LOVE NatureLovesCourage"

Terence McKenna

"*NatureLovesCourage*'s music is an outlet for the infinite sonics that traverse the Universe. Olivier has tapped into realms rarely raveled by most humans except in their dreams. One could call it New Psychedelic music or Universal Beat. If you're in need of a vacation from the absurdity called reality, book a trip on NLC's voyage".

Michael Simmons LA Weekly

NatureLovesCourage's music is pan-Gaian mana medicine for changing times; the sound of the heart opening in hyperspace"

Galen Butler

"A brilliant debut, look for great things from *NatureLovesCourage*, one of my favorite new groups"

Bruce Pavitt Sub-Pop Records

ENTHEOBOTANY
SHAMANIC PLANT SEMINARS

Psychoactive Ethnobotany

16–22 JANUARY 1999
25–31 JANUARY

Two 7-day, intensive seminars at the portal to the Palenque Mayan ruins and México's mysterious tropical forests

**Terence climbing the Magician's Pyramid in the Uxmal ruins
Mateo waits at the top.**

Post Amazon

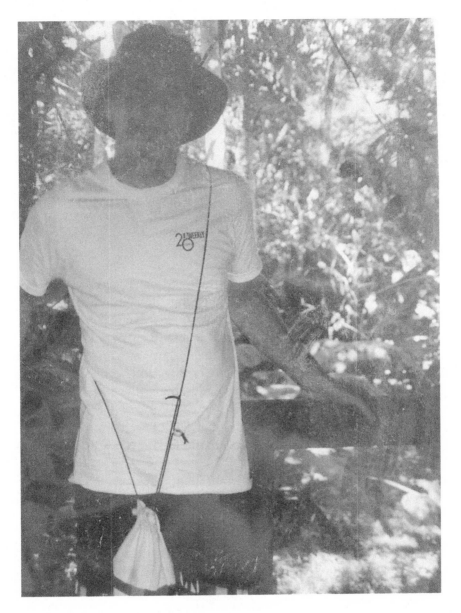

Palenque 1999

HAWAIIAN TEACHINGS

I attended Entheobotany conferences at the Mayan ruins in Uxmal in 1998 and Palenque in 1999 where I met and have stayed connected with many of my closest friends, including the editor of this book Mateo, Lorenzo of the Psychedelic Salon, Nick Doof from the early English rave scene, Anna and Sasha Shulgin, Paul Stamets, Terence and Dennis McKenna, and other fellow psychonauts who have enriched my life tremendously. It was a creative and heady time for me punctuated with deep altered state insights about myself and the nature of reality. I felt like I had transcended time to a place where I intuitively felt and predicted events looming ahead. This concept that all limitations are illusion and easily overcome is known as "Kala" in the Hawaiian tradition.

In addition to sampling and combining neurochemicals I began providing and sitting for others with these medicines starting in 1998 in Uxmal.

In Palenque of 1999 Terence heard the song "Dance Alone" which had been recorded a month before in Seattle with some friends from a band named Bonobo. Terence heard it on headphones poolside and was taken aback by what he called the lush haunting mood of the song.

"I *love it!*" was his reaction after first listening. The song has an eerie quality and the lyrics are prophetic in light of the fact that he had a Grande Mal seizure 2 months later and left the earth a year after that.

Dance Alone

"Between mind and matter there lie enchanted worlds untold
Mind conjures miracles out of time I know
The deepest part of us reveals the beauty that we are
Just as we conquer death in our mad rush to the stars
I had no idea we are leaving home
I had no idea Say goodbye
Eternal hum and rhythm is always music to my ears
Beyond the static background, I see the song so loud and clear
We come into this world completely naked on our own
The last dance you dance, you dance alone
I had no idea we are leaving home
I had no idea, say goodbye"…

DIVINATION

I was now in a phase of divination, personal transformation, and an evolution into an improved version of myself through letting go of past patterns and integrating insights gained from plant medicines like a software upgrade resulting in me following my instincts more, listening to my heart, and trusting my gut at a new level.

I attended the first of two weeks at the Palenque Entheobotanical Seminar in 1999. Mateo and I experienced 5 MEO and were eager to share the medicine. I brought a one hitter with a gram of 5MEO to the conference and turned on whoever was interested in trying it, which was just about everyone in attendance. We met in a safe room where I administered for one after another. Full breakthroughs came because I had worked out dosage and method.

Others providing NN DMT in smoked form had less success due to the fact that it took up to 3-4 deep inhalations of NN DMT. Many were unable to smoke enough of the harsh smoke to launch. 5 MEO only needs one ten milligram hit to be effective as it is 5 times as concentrated as NN DMT. I stayed on in Palenque for the second week of the conference handing off the pipe and medicine to Mateo who attended the second week, and he provided the experience to the second week attendees with similar results.

In Palenque in February of 1999 I had one of the most powerful encounters with alien fungi Cubensis of my life which brought me another complete ego death, rebirth, and transformation.

During this second week Mateo and I drank a mushroom cacao drink freshly prepared in the ancient Mayan tradition among the ruins of Palenque. P Cubensis grows abundantly in the area surrounding the pyramids and were in full flush during the conference timed intentionally by the organizer. After drinking the mushroom cacao drink Mateo and I walked to the ruins.

It didn't take long before the first wave hit, bringing that feeling of letting go and dissolving in surrender to the mushroom. The absurdity of existence and ruthless beauty of the surrounding ruins and jungle catapulted us to the edges of conscious awareness and, we split up, each wandering solo on the pyramids soaking in the rich mystical vibrations of the ruins for the next few hours.

Pure joy and raw wonder inhabited us as boundaries of time and space dissolved, leaving only the naked beauty of an exotic landscape. We met up again near a few tourists when I overheard a random conversation about human sacrifice by the ancient Mayans. Being *very high* and open to suggestion I plunged into a confrontation with my fear of death to the point of being convinced that my own death was imminent and certain to come on that very day. I remember being attracted to Sasha Shulgin"s shock of white hair as he guided attendees through the ruins.

He was not high, but recognized my state as I followed him around babbling in a mix of French, English and Spanish gibberish to which he cheerfully responded in kind. His lighthearted responses and cool demeanor helped me cope with the powerful effects of Cubensis and I saw him him as a Father Santa Claus of Psychedelics. My panick slowly subsided, but only after accepting my complete annihilation in the grips of the fungi. Although terrifying and unsettling, my life changed for the better after this intense death and rebirth experience.

All of the lyrics to the ***NatureLovesCourage*** came to me the following day while sitting by a stream. It is said that language grows where water flows and I found this to be true that day. I realized that my old self needed to die for my life to be different from what it had turned into; being a slave to debt by working a job that I was sick of after 15 years while living in Los Angeles with 15 million other people who were mostly consumed with commerce, status, and image. It was time to reinvent myself into the Artist I imagined myself to be, my authentic highest self.

I felt like Pachamama shedding her skin.

PERU DIVING DEEPER

Weeks after returning from Palenque my friend Hawk who had also been at the Palenque conference called me.

"I have prepaid for a 3 week trip to the Amazon to work with an Ayahuasca shaman and I can't go because of business. Would you like to take my place?"

I was stunned. "Let me see if I can get time off from work". I had already used up all of my vacation and sick days for the year and wasn't sure how I could do it, but was determined to make it happen. I asked my boss if I could switch switch places with an apprentice who had expressed interest in my position as production supervisor. I would take a demotion and she would replace me so I could go to the Amazon. Healing was my top priority. I had already accepted that my job of 16 years at LA WEEKLY had become my private prison and had foreshadowed the end in my mind.

Three days later I was on a plane to Peru.

After landing in Lima our group of fifteen plus the organizer of the trip met up for the connecting flight to Cuzco. On the first leg of the journey we explored the highlands of the Andes, Machu Picchu, Pisac, and other ancient sites. San Pedro cactus grows in this area and used as traditional Inca medicine as is the Coca leaf, which is chewed or consumed as a tea. Among Coca's effects is the oxygenation of the blood that makes it possible to live in high elevation without losing energy. I have no doubt that the colorful style of clothes worn by the native' is inspired by the psychedelic visions produced by the plant medicines of the area.

Many in our group tripped using LSD, 2CB, magic mushrooms or other substances while wandering the grounds of Machu Picchu, or languishing in Aguas Caliente baths in town. We also visited a local Despacho, an indigenous healer from the highlands who prepared individual bundles for each of us to offer to the Gods with prayers and intentions of healing our psychic and emotional wounds.

When my turn came to state an intention, I broke down into a sobbing mess grieving the loss of my marriage to Laura who had classic Latina features. I saw her genetics in all of the people there and the realization of why I was there in South America overwhelmed me.

I lost it, sobbing uncontrollably.

After a final day in Cusco we boarded a small plane for Pucallpa in the Peruvian Amazon, a major tributary to the Amazon.

Mother Ayahuasca

In the Amazon life is teeming with diversity and occupies every inch of the forest. Plants, animals, insects of all kinds engaged in the predatory dance of eat or be eaten.

Over the next 2 weeks of October 1999 we drank Ayahuasca five times with one day off in between sessions. Three of these sessions took place at Koriwiti retreat center near the airport on the edge of Pucallpa, a funky town on the brown muddy banks of the Amazon where all is reduced to basics and Nature has her way.

The first two nights were in Koriwiti and the next two sessions took place at the remote retreat of Hans, a German man who lived down river a few hours, and the final night we returned to Pucallpa.

All the sessions were led by Benjamin Mauro, a gentle unassuming man who was a Shipibo maestro shaman. Working with him was his Shipibo wife Amelia and a French man named Didier who lived in Peru for thirteen years and was familiar with Ayahuasca. Didier sang some Icaros in French which was special for me as French is my first language.

We began the Ayahuasca diet known as dieta a week before landing in Pucallpa. We ate lightly and cleanly with no grease spices or salt. I had been on a simple diet for all of 1999 as a result of being introduced to living foods by my friend David who also introduced me to the ancient Ayurvedic practice of urine therapy. We were encouraged to allow ourselves to simply BE, and disconnect the telephone of culture and reconnect with nature in a more focused way. The idea was to tune into instinct and dream awareness by quieting the chatter of the monkey mind and sitting with unanswered questions and being receptive and comfortable with what *is* allowing ourselves to be vulnerable, a concept counter intuitive to myself and most others in our western "civilized" culture.

The air hung thick with anticipation with the darkened maloca becoming a collective womb that we would soon be expelled from into the light of each of our individual realities created by the consequences of each of our actions that led us to this moment.

The Maloca consisted of a circular covered deck with no walls and a thatched roof and the jungle is loud, buzzing with all forms life. The constant roar of single cylinder 125cc 4 stroke engines from nearby Pucallpa served as a background to the insects, birds, and animals living in the area.

Not much happened on our first night of drinking and everyone agreed that the brew had been weak, but the second session was much different. With a new brew freshly made by Benjamin who insured its potency and quality. After stating our intentions we drank and returned to our places in the circle.

The dam burst when the sacred songs called icaros began. I felt effects of the medicine as the energy in the maloca grew louder and animated. I felt steady in the midst of the chaos for a short time, determined to keep the brew down to fully metabolize it, but in a few minutes I released a torrent of vomit from deep down in an energetic purge that left me empty and spent. Wave after wave of vomit filled my bucket until I had nothing left.

As I lay there groaning in a heap I felt a loving presence near me and smelled the sweet scent of Palo Santo, an incense made from a local tree. Benjamin spread smoke around me with condor feathers while whistling a sacred healing Mariri.

My nausea subsided and the figure in the darkness moved within inches of me with feathers rustling, softly whistling playful melodies in my ears.

Gratitude swept over me and I knew I was in the presence of love, and was in the best of care. The remainder of the session became a magical dance of light and a celebration of Being with the Mother of all plant medicines, Ayahuasca. I reveled in fantastic visionary states where all is as it should be, glistening with beauty and grace.

Down River

I spent the next day integrating and sharing insights and experiences with others in the closing of our circle which in many ways is a guided group therapy session where we learn through shared experience. After closing the circle we were left to rest up for the next session.

Our third and fourth sessions took place deeper in the jungle, about three hours by boat down the Ucuyali River, an hour out of Pucallpa. At some point in the journey our two stroke motor stopped running stranding us on the banks of the river miles from Pucallpa and our destination. We had no phone, AAA or patrols, stranded there while 4 stroke lawnmower "pecka pecka" engines kept running in boats that passed us by. In the Amazon, low tech wins.

My naive offer to swim across to river to get help from a camp was met with amused laughter. My chances of success were zero. The river was full of piranha and other dangerous creatures lurking in its murky brown depths. About an hour later we heard the pecka pecka of another boat and were able to flag them down. The thirty foot boat was already loaded down with a family, a cow, two goats and a few chickens, but they took us on board for $20, a fortune to them. We reached our destination three hours later just before sundown, giving us enough time to settle in and prepare for that night's session.

Our third session turned into one of the most powerful and transformative nights of my life. Before drinking I drew a blank at my turn to share intention so I asked for a miracle which we had been told was acceptable.

An hour after the first cup I was still baseline so I took a booster when it was offered. Right after returning to my spot I felt nauseated and grew sicker as time passed. Sweating and miserable I was unable to purge and my imagination ran away. I thought I might have malaria as I had been dropping weight since reaching the Amazon, and I had dysentery every night since drinking the brew.

Restless and uncomfortable I moaned and groaned until I heard Benjamin's voice softly call out "Jacques, come."

I managed to crawl over and sit in front of him with legs folded in a cold sweat. Greeting me with a gentle smile he applied Agua de Florida, a cheap floral cologne popular with shamans that is a mainstay in Ayahuasca ceremonies. He softly sang an Icaro to me in Quechua. Sweet notes and dancing melody poured from his heart into mine bringing me fully into the moment. I listened and watched him, realizing the importance of breath in singing. He was showing me how to breathe just by the act of singing the Icaro to me. Breathing with him had a calming effect on me and huge wave of relief and gratitude swept over me. With the realization that I loved myself enough to travel thousands of miles to the Amazon to participate in this ancient plant healing on an elemental level with this beautiful, humble, loving man who sang to me one on one in the forest with the intent of showing me how to heal myself.

This intense experience stays with me to this day. Once Benjamin saw that I had recovered and was in a good place, I returned to my space in the circle to enjoy the remainder of the session. Toward the end of the night we heard a jet engine screech directly over us, flying off into the night, startling everyone as if to punctuate the energy of the evening with a thunderous sonic boom. They told us that the CIA regularly flew from the area toward the Colombian border a hundred miles away in a cat and mouse attempt to stop cocaine traffic. I spent that night back and forth to the bathroom in a relentless dumping of old memories embedded in the shit that had been inside me.

I was cleaning house and purifying my Temple.

Over the next two weeks I purged about twenty-five pounds that I left in the Amazon to fertilize the forest. My father was alarmed when I came back fearing the worst with so much weight lost so quickly, but the truth is that I never felt lighter or clearer in my life than I did then.

The following night's session felt much smoother and easier. I had done a lot of clearing the first night and I was free to play and roam in the Emerald Crystal Forest of Love that is the magic of Ayahuasca.

The next day we relaxed on the pecka pecka on a leisurely four hour cruise up river to Koriwaiti in Pucallpa to take the Medicine for the last time, which happened to fall on October 31 1999, Dias de los Muertas, an auspicious night to end my death, rebirth, and transformation. I explored the grounds of Koriwaiti feeling light on the earth with my presence and attention highly tuned to my environment, smelling, hearing, seeing and feeling things at a deeper level than ever before. The stress of modern life had been replaced by a deep sense of calm, balance, and health over the space of three weeks.

That night after sundown we gathered in the maloca for our fifth and final session. My intention was for healing with my former wife Laura. I had written a letter to her that I mailed from Pucallpa. In it I asked for forgiveness for my behavior in the worst of times and thanked her for all the years of love and experience, and for our son Max. I let her know that I had never stopped loving her, I just had to learn to love myself better which is what I was doing in the Amazon.

The dosages and brew were dialed in at this point and the entire night went beautifully for me ending our ceremonies in spectacular fashion. The visuals came bright and powerful in the light of a full moon and the Icaros felt magical against the sound of competing sound systems that could be heard in the distance from bars a few miles away in a town full of people dancing and celebrating Dios de los Muertas. The next day's closing of the circle revealed the personal insights and healings we all had experienced and we expressed deep gratitude for the bonds and connections we made with each other and with plant spirits. We all had our shadows to dance with. Together we had faced our personal demons and deepest fears with courage and grace.

I shared a dream I had of the end of the world with our group. It starts with a tone and grows into a mix of every sound that has ever occurred into a cacophony that rises to a crescendo accompanied by an all encompassing flash of pure energy, like a lightning strike vaporizing everything, leaving only the pure presence of eternity and a total sense of Oneness in the Light of the Great Mystery that everything came from and where it all returns.

Our collective reward from the journey was clarity and a renewed sense of meaning and purpose restored to us by Mother Ayahuasca. We rested the remainder of the day and flew out of Pucallpa to Lima the following day. The seventeen hour flight to LA was comfortable. The Peruvian airline had seats that fully reclined allowing us to sleep much of the way. I remember waking as we approached Southern California from the South at night, overwhelmed at how long we flew over the sprawl of millions of people madly rushing about on an endless grid of concrete and lights with no trees to speak of, and how insane it all felt after being in the Amazon. The concrete jungle seemed more hazardous to me than anything I had experienced in Peru, and the next month in Los Angeles proved to be challenging when I found myself with all my defenses down, thrown into overload by the bombardment of a culture that I had previously thrived in.

I had shed my skin like Pachamama and was transformed, no longer in tune with the frequency and insanity of the City of Angels. The following week at work at the printers I realized that I was finished with my sixteen year career at the LA WEEKLY. The following day I told my manager that I would be quitting within months.

I essentially fired my boss and released myself from the prison I had assigned myself to for the past sixteen years. The job had served its purpose and it now held me back from experiencing the Great Mystery in its fullness and potential. I had been planning my next escape from HELL-A for a long time and now saw that my energy had to go toward stress reduction by living more in harmony with the natural world. music, minimalism, mobility, and growing food and medicine became my focus. No more deadlines, bosses, graveyard shifts or toxic environments for me. My new life included learning about natural construction, permaculture, and land stewardship.

Working with plant spirits and creating music and art were my keys to surviving and thriving in the years to come. The canvas was blank and all of the paints and brushes I needed were at my disposal along with love, support, and inspiration to help me paint my new reality. All of this happened in October 1999 and by New Years day 2000 my new life had begun.

Grandmother
"Save me a good place on the other side"
unknown

SAY GOODBYE

The Alchemical Arts Conference on the Big Island of Hawaii in November 1999 became the last conference that Terence would participate in. It was held in Hawaii to make it possible for him to attend and it turned out to be a beautiful opportunity for Terence's friends and fans to show their love and appreciation to him for one last time. Alex and Allison Grey, Tom Robbins, Paul Stamets, Sasha and Ann Shulgin, and many others spoke. Terence was physically depleted after going through experimental protocols and surgery to combat the brain tumor that had developed behind his right eye. His sense of humor, spirit, and mind were intact and his approach to his own impending demise was one of curiosity, courageousness, and inspiration.

In a state of grace and gratitude, Terence radiated and received unconditional Love, a thing of beauty to be a part of. The highly emotional charge of this gathering shook me to my core and inspired us all to another level of creativity and understanding. After his Grande Mal seizure and being saved by his girlfriend Christie, Terence's energy shifted from his mind and intellectual pursuits to his heart's emotional center. He recognized all the blessings in his life while accepting his impending physical demise. His description of a shaman as someone who has seen the End and returns to his place in life with an expanded awareness to live out his life with courage and gratitude described his state perfectly. Once someone confronts their mortality and makes peace with it they are free from fear and become empowered. NDE's are moments of grace and opportunities to re-frame reality, as are mystical psychedelic experiences.

Allchemical Arts came at the moment in time when Terence's vision of Psychedelic Community crystallized into reality. He expressed that he had come to a place of acceptance and gratitude for having been given time after his seizure to get his affairs in order and say goodbye to his family and found Psychedelic community known as the Others. The one hundred fifty attendees all had a chance to express their feelings to him at this conference and his departure and meeting with the Mystery was designed by him with full conscious intent surrounded by Love. It was here and other group events where I learned to align with my inner voice and communicate personal truths from my heart.

The outpouring of love and goodwill for Terence at Allchemical Arts was beyond anything I had ever imagined. He radiated Love fed by the full awareness of his limited time incarnate as a result of his brain tumor. Every moment felt pregnant with a magical quality of connection.

I had the honor of sitting for many attendees with 5 MEO at different times throughout the weekend, providing the medicine free in the spirit of Supreme Consciousness. The feeling of gratification I got by witnessing and providing 5MEO for people in these encounters was more than enough compensation for me. Monetizing it didn't feel right. I considered it a gift from the plant spirits. On occasion people insisted on gifting me for my time and I used this to purchase more medicine. For less than a dollar anyone can have a direct encounter with the afterlife safely and securely, and be back to baseline in 15-30 minutes, reborn and bathed in the afterglow of Cosmic Consciousness.

On the second day of Allchemical Arts I was invited to be part of a small group of people attending private sessions two weeks after the Allchemical conference in a gathering known as the Grandmother Works.

Terence McKenna

New Millennium Institute

The "Grandmother Works" were held in Waimea, Hawaii in a private home designed by Frank Lloyd Wright that consisted of 2 days of Ayahuasca ceremony followed by a session with Terence who administered NN DMT in smoked form. I had yet to experience NN DMT in smokeable form, but was well acquainted with 5MEODMT. My question to Terence "What is the difference between NN DMT and 5MEODMT", was answered without a single word being spoken.

The first day of the Grandmother session was rough for me. Terence's brew proved to be strong. The admixture of Chacruna and Ayahuasca grown by Terence on his property inspired me to coin the term Hawayahuasca to describe his brew. The organizers scheduled the sessions for mid-day with blindfolds for everyone. All my previous experiences had been at night in a darkened maloca, so this was a novel approach. Cannabis was also provided in the center of the medicine circle for anyone who wanted. I thought it unusual, but it was preferred by the people leading the group over the tradition of tobacco which the Shipibo and other indigenous shamans use.

The brew came on hard and fast and I found myself crawling to the pipe in the middle of the room to smoke herb. I couldn't refrain from making weird sounds while others purged, much to the dismay of our guides. At one point I took off my blindfold and became overwhelmed with emotion at the realization that I was sitting in a gorgeous Frank L Wright home in Hawaii, every inch of which had been designed and executed as high art.

I lost my composure and disrupted things and was counseled post session about staying in my space. I apologized to all my fellow travelers after being talked to and wanted to sit in the next two sessions without being booted out.

The second day's session went smoother than the first. I didn't take a second dose and focused my energy inward by repeating a four position Mudra shown to us before the session.

I repeated the four positions for the entire five hours of the session with as much care and discipline as I could muster which pleased the facilitators who let me attend the third session where Terence would hold the DMT pipe for the last time.

ANSWERS BEHELD

On the third day of Grandmother Works Terence arrived in a weakened state with Christie. Allchemical Arts two weeks before had left him fatigued. We met in the living room for orientation, and Terence addressed our group of thirteen by laying the ground rules for the experience.

"There are no rules except that the first person to speak is the one smoking. All others will hold space in silence during the smoker's journey".

To save time he administered two people at a time with each person facing each other on either side of him. As the first two took their positions he prepared the pipes for more.

"I advise you to very lightly kiss the glass pipe as drawing too hard is not effective. After the first hit, I will wait a minute and then ask if you want another hit. If you can hear me and get up I suggest you hit it again. I will repeat this process until you have broken through and can no longer do it. The goal is to not get stuck half baked as it were."

He handed the pipe to the first traveler and fired the bowl filled with his personal NN DMT stash, a clear rock the size of a golf ball that he shaved with a razor blade into the pipe. After smoking, each person laid back waiting for the flash to hit. A minute later Terence asked if they wanted another. Most did and some took a third before the medicine took effect. A couple of hours later after six pairs had smoked and reached various levels of DMT consciousness, Terence asked, "Did I miss anyone"?

I slowly raised my hand, "Me".

This made me number thirteen, the final person left to experience this miracle in his presence. "Come up and let's do this!"

The surreal nature of the situation hit me as I sat before him. I was about to smoke Terence McKenna's NN DMT with him in a Frank Lloyd Wright house in Hawaii after two days of drinking Terence's Ayahuasca brew. My entire psychedelic life had brought me to this moment and I decided to make the most of it by going for it with as much courage and gusto as possible.

Carpe Diem.

Terence handed me the pipe, a six-inch glass tube with a round glass bubble at the business end. He shaved about half a gram from his crystal clear golf ball of DMT and deposited some in the pipe before handing it to me. He applied a blue torch from a beautiful hand lighter to the bowl and in his signature voice said, "Now kiss the pipe".

I emptied my lungs with a long exhale and very lightly kissed the pipe filling my lungs with sacred smoke. After holding the hit for 5 seconds I exhaled and prepared for the next hit. I kissed it again and with lungs at full capacity held it. We repeated this once more and at this point I laid back holding the third hit. I was in the circus starting to enjoy fantastic colorful hallucinations when in the far distance I heard in his charmingly hypnotic nasal drall, " Do you want another hit?"

It took everything I had to sit up and I felt the pipe being held to my lips and heard the torch of the flame. As I inhaled I opened my eyes to see Terence's head and face and watched it explode into tiny fractal versions or replicas perfectly identical and spaced apart, as if I had the vision of a bee. Those tiny Terence heads morphed slowly into shiny silver reflective perfectly aligned spheres that filled my entire field of vision. The mirrored balls emitted shafts of rainbow light in all directions and rotated toward me, bathing me in the light of a *ruthlessly pure machine elf love*!!!

I was the clown *and* the circus and the joke was on me.

I stayed stunned in this encounter with Alien Love for a while and eventually came back into my body. I looked around and realized that I now sat in a different part of the room about 10 ft from where Terence sat. The look on people's faces ranged from shocked and startled to smiling and amused because I had been loud and agitated. Feeling like I might have said too much already I stayed silent, hoping to get my bearings in my body.

After an extended period of awkward silence Terence broke his own rule.

"Now *THAT'S how I SMOKE DMT!!!*"

The tension released with a roaring laugh coming from everyone including Terence who clearly enjoyed himself.

This event permanently altered me in ways I am still processing to this day. My question for Terence was finally answered and I can now say that I know the difference between the NN DMT and 5 MEO DMT experience.

What a way to end the twentieth century and begin the twenty first!

BE AWARE   BE FREE   BE FOCUSED   BE HERE   BE LOVED
BE STRONG   BE HEALED   Hawaiian Kahuna

NEW CENTURY

While attending Allchemical Arts in September 1999 I met up with Hawk, a fellow attendee and veteran of the psychedelic conferences of the late 90s in Mexico. He approached me after seeing my commitment to being a part of the events and insisted that I take $1500 from him to help me cover costs knowing that it was a stretch for me to attend these events on my income. At first I refused but he persisted, teaching me a great lesson in receiving, which I had struggled with throughout my life.

In December I returned to Big Island for the New years eve 2000 party to be held at the same Frank Lloyd Wright house where I had smoked Terence's DMT. The night was charged with a combination of excitement, anticipation and a touch of uncertainty due to Y2K, a scare that predicted the collapse of the computer world due to the resetting of clocks to 00 at rollover time of midnight. As it turned out, a real sense of change was in the air as well as a feeling of deep love and respect for Terence who would attend the gathering for the midnight festivities. At this party I would first be severely tested in my newly found role as a 5MEO DMT facilitator.

Between midnight and one in the morning on January 1 2000 in the first hour of the new millennium I was requested by my friend Mark to provide a 5MEO experience for his friends who had never tried it before. I agreed and we prepared a spot to launch near the same location that I had tripped with Terence a few weeks before.

First came John, a young man of about 30 with a curious mind and a gentle presence. He smoked and I guided him into a laying position and he went into a deep meditation like mode with a slight smile on his face. He returned a few minutes later in a state of profound gratitude and wonder after his smooth ride though eternity.

After a few minutes of post trip processing and sharing by John we moved on to Sara, his partner, a non-smoker. After trying three times we decided that Sara was unable to inhale and we moved on to her sister Mary, the last person in the group . Mary had some previous experience and was able to get a full hit. About twenty seconds in she vocalized, softly at first then progressively louder. I leaned over her and gently placed my hand on her forehead to ground and calm her, and her moans turned to screams of what looked like terror. She was clearly out of her body and unaware of the disturbance she was creating. I resorted to covering her mouth with my hand to muffle the sound because Terence was upstairs in the bedroom literally saying his last good byes to guests and friends.

Time stretched as the display of explosive energy coming through Mary went on for nearly thirty minutes before she quieted down and relaxed. It had been literally a half hour orgasm at full volume and intensity that I couldn't stop.

I subsequently made it a rule to know more about the person I sat for and to be in a less public and exposed environment to avoid this specific outcome. Mary had quieted down and returned to her body much to my relief, and to everyone's surprise she said that the experience was one of total liberation, bliss, and a sense of unity or Oneness, while on the outside she appeared to be in absolute terror.

This turned out to be a life-altering night for Mary that she was grateful for. For me it was a difficult lesson in proper screening and context when providing powerful substances like 5MEODMT to others. The karmic nature of this baptism of fire was not lost on me with the realization that I had just undergone a total reversal of roles in the DMT experience, from being the guided to the guide in the exact same spot two months later.

The week following Grandmother Works I accompanied my friend Jin An to Terence's house on the hill near Jin An's house. There beside the glowing wood stove Terence and I shared a joint and as the Hawaiians would say "talked story" including the Grandmother Works and this Great Mystery we are all a part of.

I expressed gratitude for his friendship and the opportunity to visit him in his home and smoke a joint with him. It would be the last time Terence and I spent one on one together in our bodies.

INTERSTELLAR TOUR GUIDE

Sitting and providing medicine became my work for the next few years from 1999-2006, after Terence's departure. I also became a "mushroom chauffeur" traveling the west coast in my 1973 Dodge RV dubbed Dodge City. In addition to playing and recording music, I provided and guided psychedelic experiences to people when requested which is how I started off the twenty-first century.

Terence ascended to Spirit on April 3, 2000 leaving a huge void in the world of psychedelia. In May of 2000 I returned to the Big Island to help pack the personal books of Terence's library in boxes with his brother Dennis. After sorting out the books that Dennis wanted, the remainder were sent to Esalen in Big Sur following Terence's wishes. Unfortunately those books were lost in a fire where they were stored above a restaurant in Monterey California.

When we finished boxing the last of the books Dennis left me alone with Terence's ashes on a bookshelf amid a small altar that consisted of an urn surrounded by a few items, one of which was a small green rubber frog. I saw this as a sign because my Hawaiian Spirit name was Poloka Lele or Flying Frog. I carried the 5 MEO frog medicine that day and decided it would be appropriate to have a final smoke with Terence in the realm of the Infinite.

After placing a **NatureLovesCourage** CD on the altar underneath his ashes I prepared the one-hitter with Cannabis and 5MEO. It started to rain and as the torrent grew stronger I lit the bowl and inhaled deeply, slipping into the Forever that is 5 MEODMT. A thunderous bolt of lightning struck, intensifying the experience of the launch into hyper dimensional travel, and I was in the ethers with Terence, in the afterlife. We were both at peace in the light of pure loving awareness beyond the tribulations of earthly three dimensional existence where we enjoyed each other's Presence beyond words by simply feeling. It felt that he telepathically understood my gratitude for all he had brought to my life and all of the inspiration and loving support that he exuded while on earth.

"My role is to give people permission to explore on a deeper level," was his conclusion about his life's path. He truly gave me permission to explore the depths of my consciousness for which I am eternally grateful.

The torrent of rain on the roof symbolized the tears of sadness felt for the loss of his body and it subsided as I re-entered my body. He reassured me that physical death was nothing to fear and to make the most of my time here by loving without fear, condition, or restriction. After carefully placing a necklace I had been wearing with my Mayan birthstone around the copper box holding Terence's ashes I returned to the mainland the following week to begin my new life as a portal opener and medicine carrier with 5MEO for the next six years.

Terence's ashes in his library in Hawaii

THE GREAT FALL

I awoke on the morning of 9/11/2001 and decided to smoke 5MEODMT alone for some reason. I was living in my friend's mosaic art studio on the corner of Sunset and Cahuenga in LA. Life had become pure art at this point which stretched the boundaries my imagination. I was still at the Weekly, but doors were opening, preparing me for huge shifts in my life. Since Esalen in 1997 I had attended four conferences and spent October 1999 in Peru on an Ayahuasca dieta. For me personal connection with Terence had traversed multiple dimensions including physical life and death.

I felt artistically inspired and productive while being high on a powerful cocktail of psychoactive neurochemicals. Life felt like a waking dream. I had been "sitting" with 5MEO since Palenque 1999 facilitating and witnessing hundreds of breakthrough transformations in the lives of people I barely knew as well as with all of my interested friends.

I felt like this day was a great time to imprint my new reality as it emerged. I loaded a bowl and sprinkled a fair amount of 5MEO on top, then covered it with more cannabis, and launched into hyperspace, a landscape now familiar to me. I practiced deep breathing and toning in that altered state to help ground and navigate the space better by deeply praying to Spirit. A few minutes after returning to my body my phone rang. It was my son Max.

"Did you see what is happening? The World Trade Center in New York just collapsed. Turn on the news".

I had been astral traveling on 5 MEO while 9/11 was occuring. Like the Kennedy assassination in November 1963, things would never be the same in America. I saw and felt the national mood shift to an agitated state and the idea for the song **Peace Now** came. I felt it important to ask for what we want in the coming time rather than repeating what we didn't want to achieve the optimal outcome.

It would be two years before it was written, recorded, and remixed, just in time for the first Gulf war.

PEACE NOW

Don't you ever believe the lies of his story that
Leaves out her story entirely.
Let's stop fighting each other, just live and let live
We all have the sacred right to be
Why do we wallow in misery, when we know theres a better way
Just set high intention and then follow thru
Co create a brand new day
Cause what do we want
Peace
When do we want it .
Now.
X3

Great Spirit provides for us infinitely
And earth is our mother we all love
Were all in this together
And it's time for us all to rise above
And nevermore linger in misery
cause we know there's a better way
In the heart of this darkness we become the light
Illuminate a brand new way
Cause what do we want
Peace
When do we want it
NOW.
X3

NEW PARADIGM

My last day at the Weekly meant I was ready to fly like a fledgling, struggling at first, from a steady income of sixty-thousand a year. I did not want another j.o.b. aka just over broke. I would sink or swim based on my own talents and resourcefulness with as low an overhead as I could get by with. I had already traveled and lived in a panel truck with Laura, so when my friend Joe offered to sell me his 76 Dodge 21 ft RV for $500 I moved in to Dodge City.

No more rent.

Over the next four years I travelled up and down the west coast of the USA in Lindy my new RV nickname, and chauffered and re-homed a strain of Psilocybin propagated from spores from Terence's fruiting bodies. I drove them from Olympia to LA as a service to humanity and a small income stream. I also "sat" with people and provided medicine and setting for psychonauts. I met many people at the Entheobotany Seminars through Terence who lived up and down the west coast who I now considered close friends. Among them is Bruce Pavitt, founder of Sub-Pop records and grandfather of Grunge in the Pacific Northwest. Bruce shared a similar interest in Terence and plant medicines and was in attendance at the conference on the Big Island in Dec 1999, Terence's final appearance in public. Bruce and I became close friends.

The reason I live in the paradise that is Orcas Island is because he lived here when we met and I visited him and his family on his beautiful 20 acres, another example of how Terence's influence continues to shape my life. When I met Bruce in 1999 he had already sold Sub Pop to Warner Bros and was retired, having taken to heart Terence's advice of leaving the city and living in natural beauty. Terence predicted and envisioned our current world as it is now twenty years later, eliminating the need to live close to cities. Bruce followed his lead in the 1990's by moving to Orcas.

In the first few years of the twenty-first century Bruce threw some epic psychedelic parties on his Orcas property. The approximately two to three hundred people who attended all abstained from alcohol, which always lowers the vibration. Most participants were psychedelically altered and people danced and played in the gorgeous natural beauty of the island. The love was free and unconditional with spontaneous cuddle puddles, and amazing music and vibes all around. We experimented with a new model of reality that felt like a new world and way of being. I believe the Imagine Festival was inspired by and is an outgrowth of those early parties.

My Toyota RVs on Orcas Island

ANOTHER CLOSE CALL

Almost a year after 9/11 I was commuting between the West coast and Hawaii carrying medicines not yet scheduled and available. One of them is 5MEODIPT or 5-Methoxy-diisopropyltryptamine, a sensitizer that amplifies physical sensation, allowing you to feel things below the threshold of normal consciousness. Known on the street as Foxy Methoxy, it was a substance I enjoyed and considered an ally, especially for its aphrodisiac qualities. My method of transport was a gel cap which held about 300 milligrams that I marked and mixed in with similar looking vitamins.

As the sun set I remembered to take my vitamins so I took a capsule from the jar, briefly inspected it and washed it down with some passion fruit juice thinking nothing more of it.

Within fifteen minutes a strange feeling came over me followed by the realization that I was no longer in a normal baseline state of consciousness.

The sinking feeling in my gut signaled the gravity of what I had done. I dumped the vitamins out and inspected each one, hoping to find the marked one, then panic struck.

Previous experience with Foxy showed the comfortable dose to be in the 10-15 milligram range with 20 milligrams being too much for my liking. There was little in my stomach and the effects of the roughly 350 milligram of 5 MEO-DIPT developed at a rapid rate. My heart rate increased and sensitivity to all sensory input, especially touch increased exponentially to the point of becoming unbearable. I attempted to vomit and was unable to yield anything.

After trying to vomit I knew I had absorbed the whole dose and I was in for a ride. Fear took over, turning into panic.

I instructed my friend to take me to the beach in case I didn't survive the overdose to absolve him of any responsibility. After slipping into a coma I entered a lucid dream like state where I became a disembodied Spirit traveling into the realm of deep space. As I hurtled outward I witnessed constellations and galaxies shaped like beautiful Gods and Goddesses. Without a body my fear had turned to bliss and I felt fully awake in this dream and able to navigate while remembering it all with delicious clarity. My consciousness reached the point of no return where I had to decide whether to stay among the living or move on and remain disembodied by physically dying.

At that point I came back to earth in my lucid dream where I chose to return and be in control of my movements. Passing through distant parts of the universe on the return flight I reached our solar system headed for home on the Blue planet. I rocketed past the earth's moon and tumbled end over end as I re-entered the atmosphere until I landed home. When I awoke 12 hours had passed after travelling the universe and found myself sitting in the back seat of my rental car disorientated and covered in my own puke. I had no idea who or where I was, only that I was alive and still in a body. My friend had driven me to the beach and left me to ride it out. I stumbled out of the car and made my way to the ocean to clean myself off. Being unaware of where I was I stripped off my clothes to clean myself and the police came after being called by a local resident and I was handcuffed and interrogated explaining that I "must have been food poisoned. They brought to the station to be booked and released. The charges were dropped, but the message was clear.

Kauai is *not* your home and you need to be more careful. I wrote about this experience at Sasha Shulgin's request for a book he was writing. My overdose story was evidence to him of 5 MEO DIPT having a high LDL meaning it was relatively safe with little chance of overdosing at high levels.

My next move was to return to Pele, the Big Island which represents the energy of fire, purification, and renewal. I am a Leo fire sign so this aligned with me.

BURNED OUT MAN

I attended Burning Man in 2003, 2004, and 2006, along with many other festivals in the spirit of celebration of life and art. Each successive year I stretched the boundaries of reality almost to the point of breaking, and by 2006 I had been on the multiple medicine path for 7 years, providing and administering psychedelic mind-expanding experiences to hundreds of psychonauts of all ages and persuasions. Burning Man 2006 marked a turning point for me and signified the end of my intense journey on planet earth.

On Saturday night of the 2006 Burn I dressed in full drag for fun as a way to channel my feminine spirit, complete with war paint, wig, fishnets, and heels. I danced through the crowds to techno on a cocktail of LSD and MDMA known as a Candy Flip. I felt a wide array of feelings including sexual power, vulnerability, and objectification while being physically uncomfortable in the attempt to appear sexy and attractive. It turned into a profound awakening and teaching in the things that women endure in the world every day.

As I prepared to leave on Sunday a dear friend Xavi approached me on the Playa requesting I sit for him with 5MEO. We entered a tent and as I prepared the pipe a drunk young girl stumbled in announcing that she was with him and wanted to smoke with him. Smelling disaster I advised against it and told X I would sit only for him and not his girlfriend, at least not while she was drunk. He agreed and asked her to leave.

After she left I prepared the pipe and instructed him on smoking and navigation, then I lit the pipe. Just as X he left his body, his drunk girlfriend fell back into the tent falling all over him, disrupting the session. She shouted at and ridiculed me, all the while kissing and hanging on to Xavi vying for his attention. He returned to his body in a few minutes smiling and in good spirits. It had been a disaster for me, but he seemed to be above the chaos and tripped right through it.

The feelings of humiliation and loss of control during his session forced me to examine my reality and embrace needed changes in my behavior. I was turning fifty-two and if I wanted to live long I needed to change.

Bastante is Spanish for "so much enough that it's too much."

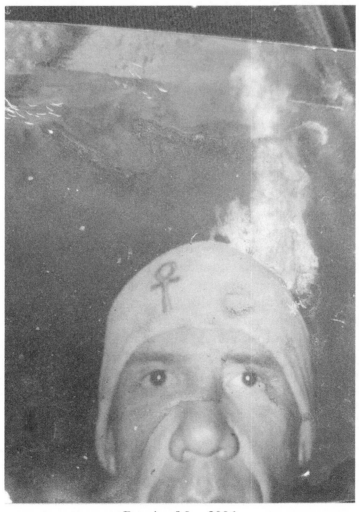

Burning Man 2006

BACK TO EARTH

My shift began in the spring of 2007 when I was offered a gig trimming weed in the mountains of Mendocino off grid on an outdoor organic farm by a friend. In my mind this was the best way for me to live the Burning Man lifestyle and not just pretend for a week.

I met Ashley in LA as I was preparing to leave for Mendocino which was totally unexpected. I was fifty-two and she was twenty-five but I figured age ain't nothin' but a number, right? She was also ready for a change in her life so I asked my farmer friends if I could bring her with me and they agreed. I had not been with a woman since my divorce in 1997 and 10 years of celibacy ended with my reawakening and reinvention.

We bonded and the summer of 2007 was heaven, living and working off grid, growing weed and organic food for the farm and living in my 4x4 Toyota RV on the edge of the garden in the hills of Mendocino. Life felt amazing and I began feeling grounded again after seven years of flying as high as I could. Ashley had a strong resemblance to Bettie Page, the pinup model from the 50s, so we decided to collaborate on an art project while on the farm. She fashioned her black hair into dreadlocks with bangs and become the character Drettie Page. Together we produced a 2008 cannabis calendar featuring her posing around the ladies, which is what we called the ganja plants.

One gorgeous day in August 2007 we did a photo shoot to the sounds of Bob Marley with her posing in and around the plants and me as photographer. I took about 100 pre digital photos and out of that shoot we chose 14 for the calendar. With our combined vision and creativity we created the Drettie Page 2008 Mendocino Ganja Calendar, which we later printed 5000 copies to sell at gigs.

HAWAII OHANA ALOHA

The following July I met Jacqueline who became my Soul Mate and loving partner for the next three and a half years. Jacquie and I knew each other in 1984 through Mitch who she was married to and I was married to Laura and still playing in the Mutts. Mitch was a hairstylist who owned a shop catering to bands and other creative's with modern eighties hairstyles using colors and radical cuts. He did my hair and Jacquie booked his appointments and took care of business for his shop, Antenna. Our first connection was a passing, platonic acquaintance.

Fast forward to 2008 when I was passing through Fairfax in northern California. I noticed a sign in a store front advertising for a hairstylist named Mitch and I realized it was the same Mitch from the eighties so I returned the next day to connect with him. During our conversation I inquired about Jacquie and he informed me that they had divorced five years earlier, but they were on friendly terms. He suggested I call her which I did the following day and we clicked on the phone and made a date for the evening of the following day. I was pleasantly surprised to find that she had lived well and looked in good physical shape. I was instantly attracted to her and the feelings were mutual. It was a relief to be with a more mature woman closer to my age who I shared a common history with. One thing led to another, we quickly fell in love for the next four years from August 2008 to December 2012 which proved to be the most wonderfully fulfilling, loving, and amazing times, as well as the most challenging and difficult period of my life.

On December 12, 2008, Obama had just been elected President, and there was a sense of optimism and positivity in the air and in my world, which became our world. While the US economy tanked, my

2008 ganja harvest went well and we were in love. There was high sexual tension between us amplified by the fact that we were both in our mid fifties.

After a few months of dating we decided to merge our lives. Jacquie quit her job of 10 years and moved to the Big Island with me to live at Terence's house where I was caretaking to help me with my music business while the Mendocino garden supported us financially. She had an impressive resume in Hollywood having worked for Rob Reiner and Norman Lear, both big name Producers in the 1980s entertainment business and while working on the Spinal Tap movie for Rob Reiner she was the test audience for the gags in the movie.

She had been without a partner or lover for over 5 years and was ready to dive in. I felt overjoyed to have a partner close to my age who was so loving and devoted. Our energy was amazing and I felt that my reality exceeded any dream or vision I ever had up to the present moment. The stars had aligned perfectly to bless me with my Soul Mate to live with in Hawaii at Terence McKenna's former home surrounded by sacred plants, a good income working for myself on my farm, and the ability to distribute my music on the Internet thanks to Jacquie's efforts. Life was a work of Art and Love ruled every day and night. We danced on the deck and tended to the garden of Eden that we lived in with love and care. My father came twice to visit and I was able to introduce him to the Real Hawaii, not just the golf tourist Hawaii he was familiar with. My son Max came to live with us and he and Jacquie who had remained childless, loved each other. I never felt more complete and fulfilled as during this period of grace and harmony.

We had it all.

Jacquie and I felt super comfortable with each other and shared lots of tenderness as well as long lingering love making afternoons to great music. After a year of being in Hawaii together we agreed we wanted to marry and started to imagine what that would look like. My 2009 harvest was successful in Mendocino and all was well in every aspect of life.

Terence McKenna in front of his house in the background
Photograph on Aluminum by Dean Chamberlain

THE FALL

Back in California the landowners of my rental in Mendocino decided to sell the property that my Ganja farm was on, so I had to find find another property to grow on. My friend Jon whom I had worked for in 2007 asked me if I was interested in a joint venture on a property in Willits for the 2010 season. After visiting the property I became an investor in the project with both finances and labor. It seemed perfect with a south-facing hillside that enabled us to grow in full sun and a big house to live in about 20 miles outside of Willits on a private dirt road. Obama had signaled that Federal resources would not be spent for enforcement of Marijuana laws and the consensus among farmers was to go BIG in 2010 as it could be the last year before legalisation changed the marijuana market forever.

It required an enormous amount of physical labor to prepare the property, including the clearing of a fair amount of trees as well as improvements to the house and clearing out cars and other things that hadn't moved for years. It was the hardest I ever worked in my life, but by July 4th the garden was ready and the plants were in place and thriving.

On July 7th a helicopter flew over and circled our new garden. This had happened every year previously. After noting it we decided it was a routine yearly census of the growers and let it go. There wasn't much we could do as we were fully committed. Jacquie flew back to Hawaii and Max and I stayed to keep working on the garden. My partners and I settled on ninety-nine plants in large grow bags on the south-facing hill, the maximum the state allowed in 2010. Our fatal mistake came from not considering the County's policy in Mendocino that allowed twenty-five plants. In this case The County's jurisdiction superceded the State and Mendocino County had not kept up with the State.

The signs were all there. The week Jacquie left a snake slithered into my RV and took up residence in my pillowcase, and a bear destroyed our chicken coop releasing and devouring all of our chickens in a bloody rampage.

At 6:00 on the morning of July 12, 2010 I heard a loud crash at the front door from my upstairs bedroom followed by a voice shouting "Get on the ground!" Eight policemen including four Mendocino Sheriffs, two Willits police, and two State Department of Justice police burst into the house machine guns and pistols drawn. Max's room was downstairs making him the first one to encounter them. My business partner Miles and his brother Ian were apprehended and handcuffed when they tried to run into the hills. Hearing the commotion from upstairs made my heart sink. My worst nightmare was happening. We had no other drugs on the property, not even any weed to smoke and seven prescriptions for 25 plants each which was required by California's medical laws. I went downstairs with my hands up and presented the documentation showing our compliance to the law in hoping they would just go away. The 2 Sheriffs were long haired biker types who were loud, chaotic, and abusive who worked mostly undercover and were clearly enjoying being bullies.

"Where's all the beer?" one shouted as he rifled through the refrigerator, "and all the other drugs?"

These "Peace officers" did whatever drugs they found while busting people and drank their beers when they found it, cowboy style. They mocked and taunted us asking questions in the hopes we would incriminate ourselves. They had invested a lot of energy into planning this bust and no amount of compliance or documentation was going to prevent them from arresting us and destroying the garden in front of us, which they did. The sixty minute ride down the hill from the farm to the jail in Ukiah sitting next to my son in handcuffs was long and depressing to say the least.

I couldn't fathom the future as I was in uncharted territory and anxious about our fate. I had invested all of my money in the farm and had not taken into account the possibility of being busted. We were being charged with felony intent to sell marijuana. One hundred and sixty plants had been counted including seventy male plants, that had been separated and left to die. After spending eight hours in a ten by ten holding tank with five other unfortunate souls we were bailed out by Mile's family and spent the night in a motel room next to the courthouse.

We had grown bold and complacent, forgetting that there were well-funded, trained groups of cops whose sole job was to track down and arrest people like me who felt that cannabis was good medicine and who believed in our right to propagate it. I discovered that the legal system generated income for the county, the jails, lawyers, judges, and police by enforcing unjust laws in a legally protected way. Those with enough money could buy their innocence and those without couldn't. The next day I sold off assets to raise funds for an attorney. Jacquie secured two loans for $7000 from her friends for my defense and Tom, a friend of mine lent me $5000. Together with the $8000 that I had raised from selling assets I had a total of $20,000 for my legal defense.

I hired Bob, a former DA in Lake County to represent us and after a year and a half of stalling the court by filing extensions and other legal maneuvers we were able to reduce the charges to misdemeanor possession of over an ounce with a penalty of 70 hours of community service for each of us and a fine of $2500. Together with legal fees it cost a total of $30,000 to stay out of jail and not have felonies for Max and I.

BACK TO BASICS

We lived in Hawaii at Terence's during negotiations with the court which became a blessing from 2008 to 2011. Jacquie and I still had each other and Max and I avoided felonies and jail time. Things were looking up once we completed community service with the worst of our legal issues over. I was able to do my seventy hours of service in Hawaii picking up trash at the old Kona airport park. The loss of financial assets due to the arrest created the necessity for us to get state assistance in the form of food stamps and Aloha Care, Hawaii's State Healthcare plan.

Jacquie and I rallied to make the best of life despite its challenges and settled into a time of deeper self-reflection regarding priorities, and what was important, which was love and connection, not money or materialism which had driven my unchecked ambition in Mendocino. We savored and celebrated our lives together bonding on a higher level than either of us had ever experienced filled with peak moments in our journey together that stay with me in the deepest depths of my Being.

My song **Source** came into being during this period. Ten years had passed since I had helped Dennis pack up Terence's books and smoked 5MEO with his ashes in his library. Jacquie and I lived in that same home when the song came to me, and Max set up his computer to record it in that same library. Within minutes the song **Source** took form, flowing smoothly and effortlessly. I wanted Jacquie to sing the chorus despite the fact that she had never been recorded before. She reluctantly agreed after I addressed her nervousness with a little encouragement. She got into a flow and enjoyed the process and experience. After recording guitars and vocals, Max added rhythm and synthesizer patches to produce **Source,** my favorite song. We collaborated on the lyrics :

SOURCE

We all belong to the Source of Creation
You become the song you sing and it becomes you
When water flows long enough even rocks will wear through
You become the songs you sing as they become true
And love sweet love is all that is you
We become the songs we sing as they become true
And if water flows long enough even rocks will wear through
We became the songs we sang as they became you
And love, love is all that is true

Jacquie and Hoku on Terence's deck in Hawaii

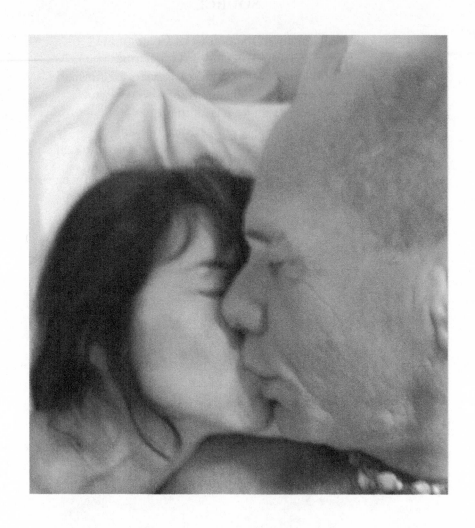

THE UNTHINKABLE

After a routine blood test Jacquie discovered that she had Hepatitis C amidst an epidemic of Hepatitis C diagnoses, something that can lay dormant for many years. Many Baby Boomers shared needles when shooting drugs in the 1970s and Jacquie had experimented with heroin in her 20s which now came back to haunt her. Max and I were tested as suggested by doctors, but we had not contracted Hepatitis. Further testing discovered two tumors near the portal vein of her liver, which was devastating news. Jacquie's mother had died in the hospital while getting a biopsy of a tumor at age 56, so we approached the tumors assuming they were malignant, treating them the way Jacquie wanted.

She researched liver cancer and began a protocol of nutritional therapy that incorporated the Gerson method while taking other supplements. When word got back to her eX-husband about this he encouraged her to return to California to have a biopsy done on the tumors. I worried because Mitch had been passive aggressive toward me and seemed jealous of Jacquie's happiness. He wanted her to stay with him while she got biopsies done in California. Our stressful situation brought out many raw emotions between us and in June Jacquie decided to go to California to visit her friends and get a biopsy of the tumors.

A week after she left Hawaii I went to California to support and be with her. She informed me that she was staying at Mitch's apartment and that I was not welcomed there. He seemed resentful of me and blamed me for Jacquie's illness.

When I arrived in California she was in the hospital getting the biopsy. I picked her up from there to bring her back to Mitch's. She looked like she had aged 20 years in two weeks. She was extremely weak and told me she had been tricked into getting biopsies by Mitch and the doctors who told her it was the right thing to do. She never wanted to disappoint anyone and was doomed to repeat her mother's fate.

I had a buyer interested in my 4x4 truck in San Diego and decided to go there to sell it to raise money for a health clinic in Arizona that Jacquie had researched. The biopsy took a lot out of her and caused the tumor to grow faster, so I drove to San Diego the next day from Marin. When I left her I said "You know I love you forever Jacquie".

She replied "and I love you forever Jacques."

Those were our last words to each other.

Near Santa Barbara I got a call from Mitch saying that Jacquie was in hospice and declining quickly, so if I wanted to see her alive I needed to return to Marin right away. Stunned, I turned around and drove North , non-stop to Marin, arriving at midnight to find Jacquie deep in an opium-induced slumber. After sleeping on the floor under her bed I awoke in the morning hoping to communicate with her. I bent over and whispered in her ear that I was there and that I loved her and she stirred.

Mitch prepared a syringe to administer morphine he had been giving her for pain. I asked him to wait a minute so that I could communicate with Jacquie and he flew into a rage screaming at me and blaming me for her condition and situation. He ordered me to leave and slammed the door behind me and returned to give her what turned out to be a lethal dose.

Jacquie left her body later that night of July 12, 2011 exactly one year to the day that I had been arrested in Mendocino. Words fail to describe the depth of loss and sorrow I felt which only grew as the hours, days, weeks, months, and years passed.

WOUNDED WARRIOR

After my soulmate Jacquie ascended I went into a prolonged state of grief, and left my caretaking position at Terence McKenna's house in Hawaii where we had lived for three blissful years. I had restored the house and garden which had been neglected since Terence's passing in 2000. Our labor of love included sanding and refinishing all the wood surfaces including a large deck where we spent hours lounging and dancing. I removed rust that had overtaken the spiral staircase to the upstairs library and repainted it along with the rest of the walls in the house, and I planted fifty new Chacruna cuttings and maintained other medicinal plants, then I cleaned the inside of a giant water tank and did other needed maintenance..

After selling and giving away other possessions I moved out of Terence's house with Hoku and Baba, two Staffordshire pitbulls in October of 2011. I moved into my flat black 1983 Suburu wagon and went to the northern tip of Big Island where King Kamehamea came from because of the superior air quality and I based myself in the Hawi, North Kohala area car camping at local beaches where I played my ukulele while singing and crying every day. Performing live music at the farmers markets in South Kona and North Kohala became a sacred prayer for me and an opportunity to channel my feelings through sound and heal my broken heart.

NEW HOME FOR BABA

In November of 2010 while walking the dogs at Puako harbor a local man named Jim asked if he could pet Baba, Hoku's beautiful brindle brother. Jim told me that his beloved family dog had passed three months earlier and he was thinking about getting another to live on his fifty acres in Puna with his family of three kids. He and Baba connected right away and I had been struggling with two pitbulls in a Suburu wagon, so I offered Baba to the good home he deserved. Thrilled Jim offered me $50 as a token payment which I accepted. I knew his sons would be overjoyed and I was certain Baba would have a great life on Jim's farm which left Hoku and I with a simpler life.

I car camped until the Suburu gave up the ghost in August of 2012 when I befriended a caregiver named Eliza who let me use her Prius in return for helping her get to a physical therapist to recover from a broken leg she had suffered a month earlier. Sleeping in her Prius was tricky which I did when it rained. Otherwise I slept on the beach.

E HO MAI

In October of 2012 I became part of a traditional Hawaiian Hale building project under the supervision of Kumu Uncle Walter and the project had a profound impact on me.

Hale is a term for a structure built by ancient Hawaiian people that incorporates no metal, secured with lashes woven from coconut strands. Uncle Walter substituted nylon parachute cord for coconut husk for lashes on our Hale to comply with building codes to secure the joints. Everything else was done in the ancient traditions of the Order of Ku builders and defenders in Hawaiian culture.

I became the eldest and the only haole, what Hawaiians call white people in the group. We did Kava ceremonies while learning chants and rituals honoring the Spirits of the land called the Aina and the forest ancestors to ask permission to harvest for the Hale. Every act was playful, yet sacred in the building process. The entire experience immersed me into Hawaiian ways and it is an honor to be accepted and welcomed as Ohana meaning family by dear cousins and nephews of Kohala. Our project gave me structure and a goal to work toward as a team member and I became certified as a Hale builder in the Order of Ku builders and defenders of the Hale. I also have the love and respect of my Hawaiian Ohana which I reflect back to them. I used the words of the Hawaiian chants *E HO MAI* and *E ULU* as lyrics that I put to music that I wrote and recorded when I came to the mainland in early 2013.

The ritual of Kahului, meaning corner, is a martial art accompanied by a Hawaiian chant performed whenever a stranger approaches the Hale while it's being built. Its function is to determine the intent of the stranger and depending on that intent, either to invite them to join in building or attack and kill them in a series of powerful moves and positions. We were all required to learn the Kahului well enough to lead the group in this art. I still practice the moves and chants whenever I need to summon my Mana or personal power.

Maui was the site of a winter solstice gathering I attended which included Ram Dass as a guest speaker. At dusk on December 20, 2012 I drank some Hawayahuasca that had been grown at the property of a friend and took a solo journey with Hoku as my companion in the gentle Hawaiian forest. This was also the end of the Mayan Calendar when Terence McKenna's Timewave Theory predicted a condition of maximum Novelty, creating a defining moment in history seen as a quantum leap in the evolution of our species on what would have been 1 month after his sixty-fifth birthday.

December 21 was the first day of a Solstice weekend on the grounds of Dr.Lou's beautiful Ocean front Maui home where we participated in Sacred Ceremony, Dance, Music, and Arts to celebrate Winter Solstice. Ram Dass was the featured speaker, but had few words to say as a stroke had affected his speech. The long silence between his words seemed to connect the group in a dramatic and beautiful stillness at that peaceful moment in time.

Early on that first day a strong wind picked up on the cliff's edge blowing a 30 foot dome over like a kite, blowing it into the ocean. Someone gave me a Leatherman knife and told me to cut the lines holding the canvas to stop this from happening. When I reached to cut the line, a gust of wind jerked the dome resulting in me cutting off the tip of my left thumb. After coming down from the ladder I recovered the chunk of thumb and put it in my pocket and concentrated on stopping the blood that gushed everywhere. We tied it off and went to the Hospital where it was sewn back together three hours later.

I returned to the gathering in time for the opening ceremony to see the dome was safe and secured. About three hundred people attended with a loving, electric feeling in the air. My friend Tara handed me a device designed to accelerate healing of wounds through UV lightwave and pulse technology. She pointed out to me that many indigenous cultures had engaged in the practice of flesh offerings for the recently deceased as a form of respect, making me conclude that this was my flesh offering to my Beloved Jacquie. I think the Healing Light was effective because my thumb appeared to heal quickly.

It can be argued that by the Winter Solstice 2012 the world was a different place than ever before with the emergence of the Internet and cellphones in an unprecedented leap in how the world works and how people relate, communicate, and behave. Big Tech has algorithms that put Artificial Intelligence or AI in charge of our behaviors in a new way giving more credibility to Terence's Timewave theory that predicted the date as the beginning of a steep descent into novelty.

Hale at Iole in Kohala

BLESSINGS AND MANIFESTATIONS

Upon return to Kohala and the Big Island we completed the finishing touches on the Hale at Iole. A large part of the community of Hawi and Kapaau turned out for the blessing by the Kahunas and Tribal elders of the Big Island as is customary in Hawaiian culture. It was a joyous occasion and many in the community had participated moving lava rocks, harvesting fan palms and lashing the roof over a three month period. My experience of building the Hale with Hawaiians was meaningful and healing to me during that time in Hawaii, making it truly one of my Spiritual homes.

IKE   The world is what you think it Is
KALA   There are no Limits
MAKIA   Energy follows Attention
MANAWA   Now is the moment of Power
ALOHA   To love is to be happy with.
The joyful sharing of life energy in the present.
MANA   All power comes from Within
PONO   Effectiveness is the measure of Truth. All Good.

RETURN TO MAINLAND

My father had health issues on the mainland so I left Hawaii to spend time with him and assist in whatever way I could in his caretaking. He had elected to have corrective eye surgery in his right eye, but it didn't go well and caused him great discomfort in the form of watering and itchiness making it impossible for him to golf, one of his favorite activities. His chronic discomfort led to depression and the beginning of the end of my father's will to live over the next year. In early 2013 Hoku and I left Hawaii to be closer to where he lived in Laguna Hills, California. I had been playing and writing music in Hawaii and recorded simple arrangements of ukulele and vocal tracks with Tom Mansour, a friend who was a lifeline to earth in my deepest times of grief and despair. We recorded the first week after I returned to LA in one session when my emotions were still raw.

My father's wife Phoebe had put him into a caretaking facility when it became too demanding for her to meet his needs which caused him to feel lost and disorientated until he developed symptoms of Alzheimer's disease. He passed peacefully on January 4, 2014, breaking my heart once again while I was recovering from the loss of Jacquie. He had lived a long and good life at 87, but his last two years were difficult for everyone.

Aloha Ho

I loved my father deeply and am grateful for the times we had together in Hawaii. On our first trip in 1970 when I was 15 and coming of age, we golfed every morning and cruised the hotel bar after dinner. I am pretty sure that once I was in bed he returned to the bar to womanize, something he was known for. We lived the Golf tourist version of Hawaii that he knew and loved and for me the trip was transformational. I vowed to live there after I got off the plane and felt the warm trade winds caress me with the sweet scent of plumeria.

In 2004 my dad and I met up in Kauai and flew to the Big Island where we went into a recording studio and laid down tracks on which he crooned in his deep rat pack piano bar voice singing, "Aloha Ho Aloha Ho until we meet again Aloha" over and over to a ukulele track. Ho was short for Jorge, George my favorite nickname for him which also meant prostitute in street lingo. I later added vocals and other instruments digitally capturing a sweet moment in the one and only recording experience of his life. Ten years later in Jan 2014 I played the track at his eulogy and relived the moment of his vocal presence along with everyone else there who never heard it before.

Dad visited me twice in 2009 and 2010 while I was caretaking Terence McKenna's home and garden on the Big Island and I had the pleasure of introducing him to the real Hawaii away from the resorts and tourists on the mauka, mountain side of Mauna Loa, one of three active volcanos on the Island. Nestled deep in a Ohia forest the house is on 5 acres of botanical paradise and features a large front deck where George, Jacquie, Max, Hoku and myself spent most of our time when not at the beach or on some other adventure, Goddess Pele's home.

My memories of these times are some of the most fulfilling and precious of my life. All of my dreams had effortlessly manifested to fulfill every desire and to connect me emotionally with the closest members of my family forty years after my first visit and fifty years after my father's first visit in 1959. George and I played our final round of golf together with French actress Claudine Longet in 2010 to complete the circle of the Hawaiian experience together, the same way we started.

Stroke of Luck

In April of 2014 I became involved in a friend's ganja farm in the hills above Santa Barbara. The property was over grown and required extensive clearing before we could grow there. I worked in hot weather laboring on the land that day and became dehydrated, and while taking a break I suffered a stroke that made me lose my entire left side in motor function. I had no pain, just a sudden loss of control over the left side of my body and some brain fog.

After confirming the stroke in an LA hospital the next day, I was left to recover and rehabilitate on my own as I was uninsured and broke. The loss of my left side made it impossible to play an instrument which left me in an existential void. Who was I without the ability to express myself musically? This motivated me to practice every day to regain my musical skills. Slowly I formed chords with my left hand and completely relearned technique on ukulele and guitar. Fear of loss and purpose drove me in regaining my musicality, and it took over a year to recover the fundamental ability to play again.

I credit my canine companion Hoku with my recovery and saving my life after Jacquie and my dad George crossed over. The demands of a young pitbull required constant vigilance and physical interaction.

I had dedicated my life to Hoku when I realized how intense she was in Hawaii and the level of responsibility a pitbull like her required. After walking her a few miles a day for three months I regained my ability to walk normally. It took more than a year to relearn how to play guitar and ukulele but persistence, a sense of purpose, and Hoku inspired me to plow ahead and regain my left side. Her love and companionship connected me to life in a real and immediate way, and I eventually regained about ninety percent use of my body although I had lost some life force.

The slow decline and passing of my father combined with the restrictions placed on my visits broke my heart again just as I was recovering from the grief of Jacquie's sudden departure. After my stroke I felt that highly emotional states of mind can trigger events like strokes when heart dis-ease is present, that it was possible to die of a broken heart which is what happened to me.

Dad and me

GREAT ESCAPE 3

Max left Hawaii after Jacquie passed and returned to LA to stay with his mother Laura and her boyfriend Eric. Laura was having some physical issues that first appeared in 2012 as a loss of balance and the use of her right arm. They turned out to be symptoms of ALS, amyotrophic lateral sclerosis or Lou Gehrigh's disease, a fatal condition of the nervous system. Max, Laura, and Eric moved in together but the chemistry between Max and Eric became toxic.

Laura declined quickly which is what happens with ALS. People typically die within four years after their symptoms first appear. Max and I had to convince Laura to leave Eric who was strung out and not helping things in any way.

In January 2015, one year after my father passed, Laura agreed to come with me so I could care for her full time. We had been divorced for seventeen years, but our bond was deep because of Max and now we would be together again. I had mostly recovered from my stroke and felt prepared for our second Great Escape. In early February 2015 I drove to LA and picked Laura up, literally, as she was now confined to a wheelchair and largely immobile. Thirty-six years had passed, we had been married, divorced, and had a son since our first Great Escape in 1979. Her Spirit was broken as she had lived in squalor due to Eric's lack of care.

A drowning man can save no one.

We got in my camper and drove South to spend time with her brother whom she had not seen in ten years. A river of tears flowed when we reconnected with Al and Laura's mother Thelma. Years of resentments and disappointments were released in the face of our circumstances. With ALS those afflicted initially suffer a loss of balance and motor sills followed by a gradual shut down of bodily functions. The mind is not affected leaving the person fully conscious as they lose motor functions leading to death usually within 5 years of onset. Physicist Steven Hawking was the longest known high profile survivor of ALS having reached his 60's before succumbing to it.

Care-giving someone with ALS is challenging as they can do very little for themselves. They are literally immobilized until they lose the ability to speak. I was determined to make Laura's remaining time on earth as good as possible by dedicating myself to her. After visiting her mother and brother in San Diego we drove North on 101 Highway to Ukiah in Mendocino County where I had grown ganja six years before, retracing our first Great Escape from 1979.

Laura's Birthday

Max and Laura

For the first month in Ukiah we stayed in a cheap motel out of necessity while searching for something more permanent, then a lead from a friend named Eric got us a studio apartment in a beautiful part of Ukiah, which became a blessing. I am eternally grateful to Eric for helping us in our time of need. Sometimes it's the people we most recently meet who come to our aid over those we have known a long time.

I was able to get help with Laura after about six months of solo care-giving and hitting the burnout wall common to caregiving in our situation. I hired Celia as a caregiver for some relief and she and Laura bonded while I got a few hours to myself, something essential for good caregiving.

This became a period of healing and forgiveness for us both. We were able to reconnect and share the remainder of Laura's life with our son who visited often. By October Laura lost her ability to speak and we communicated through blinking once for yes and twice for no. I considered it an honor to be present for her in her final days, which were fast approaching. Laura, Max, his partner Ashley and I went to a theater in Ukiah on New Years 2016 to watch the newest Star Wars movie. The first Star Wars came out when we first met in the 70s and this would be our final event together.

I had trouble falling asleep on the evening of Jan 5. 2016. My song **Source** played seemingly on its own at around 2am on my computer. I let it play through and closed my computer, then went to sleep waking up at 5am to find that Laura had stopped breathing and left her body while I slept. After attempting to revive her, I realized she was gone, so I called 911 who sent an ambulance. It is said that there is a disruption in the electrical matrix when a soul leaves their body and since we are electrical beings there is a shift when an electrical charge is disrupted in a room. When I tried to turn on my computer the next day nothing happened. The logic board had failed at the time Laura had crossed over, sending her off, serenaded by my song **Source**.

I called Max and together we mourned our loss. Even though we all knew that her time was limited, it didn't lessen the impact of her death on us. Laura was the third person close to me to cross the veil in a short period of time. No matter how many times we grieve it is always a powerful, bittersweet, and personal experience that reminds us of our own mortality and vulnerability. Crying became a welcome friend releasing emotion and not holding back from expression. It is always a relief to let go and embrace raw feelings as they flood you being in the grip of grief, and me crying deeply eventually morphs into laughter and vice versa.

They are two sides of the same emotional coin.

It is important to reach out for support when death strikes to stay connected to the living. I am fortunate to have friends who listened to my ramblings without judgment or advice, to simply be present for me in the depths of my sorrow.

Mahalo brother Wells Jones.

Death is a powerful teacher and one lesson it teaches is non-attachment. Nothing lasts and everything passes in time. It is best to stay in a state of conscious loving awareness as much as possible, not to fear death, but to embrace it as part of the natural cycle of life.

David Bowie died the week after Laura followed by a succession of other well-known musicians within a few weeks of each other. Laura was to be the third person close to me to ascend after Terence in five years. Once again my life became an open canvas with no responsibilities except to Hoku and myself.

Change was once again in the air.

POST PARTUM

I landed a growing gig in Humbolt County in March of 2016 for the outdoor cannabis season. The quickly changing landscape of the cannabis market made it one of the last years to grow weed. I also secured work for Max and his partner Ashley allowing them to move and create a new reality for themselves after Laura passed. Being in the remote mountains of Humbolt proved to be good medicine for us with our focus on plants, earning money, and savoring the connection we made with new found friends.

The following year in 2017 I negotiated an agreement with an old friend to do a small grow on his property near Eugene Oregon. For this last crop I personally prepped, planted, grew, harvested, cured, trimmed and packaged twelve large plants in a greenhouse which came out to a perfect seven pounds. I sold ounces to friends of top-shelf bud for less than dispensary prices in what became a one-time project and fitting conclusion of my pot growing career.

In November of 2017 I was invited to a Medicine circle at the same place I had first experienced Ayahuasca in 1998 twenty years before with Don Jose, a shaman from Peru. My life had been filled with challenges since 2011 and didn't feel I was ready for the ordeal that was Ayahuasca, but I did feel ready to unburden the grief from all the loss I had experienced. I was cautious out of respect for the Medicine and offered to sit as a helper in the sessions without drinking to be present for those who might need assistance in the ceremony. The original organizer of the circles since their inception in the eighties had turned over duties to a new organizer who had been with the circle for years. After his 85th birthday on advice from his cardiologist he was no longer physically able to participate. Working with Mateo and another musician named René gave me an opportunity to contribute to the circle without getting high. Mateo and Jeff the organizer invited me to contribute to the soundscape with musical offerings of ukulele and an Icaro I had learned in the Amazon in 1999. The sessions were successful and highly appreciated by attendees. I was impressed with Jeff and Mateo's skills in organizing the sessions so on the third night I drank a third of a dose to ease into the medicine. I wanted to be altered, in tune with the participants while being present enough to conduct the ceremony properly.

After my initial nausea the brew kicked in bringing gorgeous glistening visual enhancement of energy fields that surrounded others as they approached the alter for a booster dose. I believe that DMT allows us to see more of the electromagnetic spectrum than in a normal waking state which can be seen as an overlay of shining energy that has been hidden. I realized that I was too high to participate in guiding the ceremony so I relaxed and enjoyed the ride until I was able to regain my bearings, then I contributed a simple but beautiful offering on the ukulele for the group. Even this act felt miraculous to me in that moment. Around an hour into the session I settled in to a perfect zone of being altered enough to facilitate while still being entranced by the Mother's gifts, making a perfect reconnection to the medicine after years of absence from that world. It brought me full circle from the first experience in 1998 when I wanted to contribute musically. Now I participate in circles every spring and fall as a part of my spiritual practice and my way of praying and staying connected to plant spirit and Supreme Consciousness.

OH CANADA

My next move was to continue North to Canada to renew my Canadian Passport which had expired in 2009. I had little to no restrictions or commitments and thoughts of traveling and exploring felt appealing. I went North to Orcas Island to visit my long time friend Bruce and others. Orcas is only two ferry rides to Victoria Canada where the Passport office is. I also dropped off a few applications for work thinking of possibly living on Orcas.

My RV lifestyle gave me the flexibility of mobility, and Orcas Island is as peaceful and healing a place as can be found on the planet. Its charm and pristine environment, plentiful pure fresh water and great community made it the perfect place to write this book. This magical gem of an island is as far north as one can get in the USA besides Alaska.

After securing my passport in Victoria on my sixty-fifth birthday in August, I was offered work at Island Market on Orcas. I went back to Orcas and integrated into the community. After switching jobs to the Co-op market I got into a great flow and began writing this memoir.

I have fond memories of 2018-2019 which should have been the final year of my life on earth. I had designed a low stress life where I felt supported and valued by a community surrounded by and embedded in a beautiful environment. I felt content and at home even without a home living in my two Toyota RVs on the Island. In August 2019 I sold my four wheel drive Toyota camper that I had tried to sell when Jacquie fell ill in 2011, and with that money I custom ordered a Taylor twelve string guitar built in October of that same year.

IMAGINE

I felt an urgency to play the Imagine festival on Orcas Island in September of 2019 and got a musical booking there for Friday September 13, 2019 on a full moon.

I half-jokingly told Darin, the force behind Imagine that he should book me because at sixty-five, "there might not be many more opportunities left to do so."

The evening of September 13, 2019 turned out to be a full Harvest Moon on Friday the 13 where I was "prayerforming" as NatureLovesCourage in the Revival Tent at the festival playing a set that my friend Fabrice and I had rehearsed for the previous three months. We started at eleven on Friday, the first night of the festival. About 50 people had gathered to see us making it an intimate affair, my preferred audience. I handed Fabrice a microdose capsule of lions mane and .25 grams of psilocybin which we both took with the intention of feeling their gentle effects as the set was ending.

We began with a Sanskrit chant performed with music called **Ohm** Burbuva Swaha to set intention and mood. The next song was a Sacred Hawaiian chant, **E Ho Mai** that means Bestow Unto Me a song I had written music to. We were off to a great start, next came **Island Style**, a popular Hawaiian song that is uplifting and funny, which set the stage for the rest of the show, then we played John Lennon's **Imagine** which the Festival was named after followed by **Suddhosi Buddhosi** a Sanskrit lullaby and IZ's version of **Over the Rainbow,** a crowd favorite.

A large heart had been painted above the stage where we finished the set with the song "**Lazy**" by David Byrne of Talking Heads. Before the song I looked at Fabrice and in a mushroom flash telepathed to him my pleasure and gratitude for him, the music, and how we were being received and loved' when we began the song ***Lazy***.

The lyrics go like this

"Im lazy when im lovin Im lazy when I play
Im lazy with my girlfriend a thousand times a day
Im lazy when im sleepin   im lazy when I talk
Im lazy when im dancing and im lazy when I walk
I open up my mouth air comes rushin out
Nothing doin nada never how u like me now
Wouldn't it be mad, wouldn't it be fine
Lazy lucky lady dancin lovin all the time
Im wicked and im lazy
Ooohh don't you want to save me   repeat

Well some folks they got money and some folks lives are sweeter
Some folks make decisions and some folks clean the streets
Imagine what it feels like imagine how it sounds
Imagine life is perfect and everything works out
No tears are falling from my eyes   I'm keeping all this pain inside
now don't you wanna live with me
Im lazy as a man can be
Im wicked and im lazy
Ooohhh don't you want to save me repeat

Imagine there's a girlfriend imagine there's a job
Imagine there's an answer   imagine there's a god
Imagine im the devil imagine im a saint
Lazy money lazy sexy lazy outer space
No tears are fallin from my eyes
Im keepin all his pain inside
Now don't you wanna live with me
Im lazy as a man can be
Im wicked and im lazy   ooohhh don't you wanna save me   repeat
"Hard   man,   hard   lives   Hard   keeping   it   all   inside
Good   times,   good   God,   *So   lazy   I   almost   stopped*"

At that moment my chest felt as if I was crying deeply and the word

Surrender filled my mind. My heart stopped and I collapsed. Fortunately for me, Mel Seme of the headlining band GoneGoneBeyond was in the audience and dove to break my fall, preventing my head from hitting the ground.

I had a full-blown cardiac arrest as I had literally played my heart out in front of the people who bore witness to my death on stage. Many in the audience thought my collapse was a part of the show and I was faking it as part of the performance. Luckily others in the audience recognized the reality and sprang into action.

Someone ran to get Tracia, a nurse proficient in CPR who was on staff for this possible scenario. I lay there lifeless for close to two minutes until Tracia arrived. When she checked I had no pulse or heartbeat and my skin had gone pale and was growing cold. She sprang into action with a determined aggressive CPR technique and cracked my ribs to have better access to my heart. I was told she shouted at me, completely focused on reviving me. "Not on my watch!" she screamed as she pumped my chest keeping blood circulating to my brain and body.

Without her passion and heart I would not be alive today and where others might have given up, she persisted. After 10 minutes of CPR she shocked my body *six* times with electric paddles. They told me that at the sixth jolt I let out a scream and sputtered back to life reanimated from the infinite void of non-embodiment. Tracia stayed with me until the EMT'S arrived.

After collapsing it felt like my body had powered down like when you shut off your cell phone. All went black and there was total silence and stillness like entering limitless empty space. My consciousness began to adapt and appreciated the total freedom of no body. The constant maintenance of life in a body was no longer required. Complete peace and freedom with no restrictions. A funny thought entered my mind. "If this is eternity, it could get boring after awhile," then I awoke back in my body.

The first thing I remember seeing was a crowd of EMTs preparing to load me into the ambulance while asking me questions to determine the state of my consciousness. I said "I'll be ok, I can't afford a $4000 helicopter ride." That amused and relieved everyone there witnessing the drama of my literal death and rebirth. They took me to the airport, loaded me into a helicopter, and flew me to St. Joseph's Peace hospital in Bellingham where I was admitted and stabilized in the Emergency room.

I later learned that the percentage of people who survive similar heart attacks is five percent with many of them suffering brain damage, rendering them into a vegetative state.

After experiencing what is called a "Widowmaker" heart attack I agree that it is the most appropriate term, given my history of personal loss in recent years.

During the ambulance ride the EMTs took bets on my survival with most betting against me. Fortunately for me they lost their bets and I became a true one percenter without the fortune, but certainly the most fortunate man alive.

"All you touch and All you see
Is All your life will ever Be"

Pink Floyd

HELICOPTER RIDE SELFIE

REANIMATION

As a musical creative I know of no greater high than being *on* stage in a live musical event fully engaged with the audience, especially when they participate and connect on a deep personal level.

My friend Mel is a musician in the band GoneGoneBeyond who made the diving catch that prevented my head from hitting the ground when I fell. Tracia is the nurse proficient in CPR who was in an adjoining tent, ready with her shock paddles for emergencies.

These 2 preconditions were a miracle. In normal circumstances the survival rate for a full blown heart attack is five percent. On an island with no hospital or emergency services is less than one percent. Contemplating all of this a year after it happened I still found it difficult to wrap my mind around. The only part I played was knowing deep within me that I *had* to play and share my love with musical prayers at Imagine in 2019. I literally played my heart out in a cosmic dance as did everyone else involved for all of us to have this experience, and that is the beauty of Life. Every One and Everything was essential for the dance of my life to go on for me.

In hindsight I realize that I had been withdrawing from attachments and people leading up to Imagine, preparing for and writing my own swan song. An overall feeling of irrelevance overtook me and although grateful for my life and the natural world, I secretly felt that my time had come and gone and at sixty-five my best days might be behind me and it was time to let go and join the spirits of my loved ones on the other side of the Veil. I began writing this book in September 2018 intending to chronicle the events of my life so others could have a taste of it after I departed, but now this book has become a celebration and triumph of life and love highlighted by my perfectly designed death and miraculous reanimation.

At Imagine 2019 audience participation went to the next level. Not only did they sing along, they witnessed and participated in my death and rebirth. I believe I had subconsciously imagined and orchestrated my own death in a setting that made it possible for me to allow my life to be saved by love as a result of doing what I love most; sharing loving intent through sound.

Talk about audience participation.

Perfect timing is what we all know is Everything. The universe and stars were in full harvest moon alignment and there was a moment of grace where everything was perfectly harmonized in me so I could literally die and be reborn in that exact moment in time.

This is the final chorus of David Byrne's *Lazy* that I never got to:

"I'm wicked and I'm lazy
OooHHH don't you want to Save Me."

FROM THE OUTSIDE

The following are three accounts of what occurred that night from the perspective of others who witnessed and participated in the miracle of my survival. The first is from Mel Seme, the musician from Gone Gone Beyond who headlined the festival that weekend. Mel had been in my audience and sprang into action. The next is from Darin who booked and managed the Imagine festival, and the third is from Tracia, the lead nurse who administered CPR and shocked me back to life.

Mel stated, "I was watching you perform and you stopped, I saw that you were losing consciousness and as you collapsed I dove to prevent your head from hitting the ground, barely breaking your fall. I held your head on my lap while others went for help which was miraculously very close by. After a minute or so your heart stopped and the weight of your head suddenly felt like a bowling ball in my lap.

Your body went limp and was lifeless for over two minutes until Tracia arrived and began CPR. Not until the sixth shock from her defibrillator paddles did the electrical life force return to your body. Her energy was intensely charged with Love and focus on bringing you back to the living".

Darin, the Imagine festival organizer said, "I've known Jacques for 15 years now. He has always been a mystical character that has popped in and out of my life over the years. In my time producing shows one of the things I remember was when I had just produced a pretty outrageous psychedelic event. I was cleaning up afterwards still high on LSD. Jacques walked in with his ukulele and played for me as I cleaned up alone. It was a beautiful moment that stayed with me. Knowing that Jacques had a history with some of the Premier Psychedelic heads of our time, I was happy to have him join us for a number of our events. This time at Imagine we had him playing on a stage in the Revival tent and I came by to see his performance. I watched him play a song as the crowd sat and enjoyed the music. I walked away for a few minutes and about five minutes after I left the tent I got a call on the radio that someone had just passed out. By the time I ran back to the stage area Medics were there and had begun clearing everything and tearing his shirt off. Jacques had passed out on the stage at the end of his music set and was now lying there without a pulse. I had a moment of panic as I realized that he may have died onstage.

The medics kept doing chest compressions and hooked up an Automated External Defibrillator or AED that made beeping sounds as everyone was told to stand back when it shocked him. He still had no pulse so they continued with the chest compressions. I stood there and watched as this surreal moment unfolded. Jacques still onstage getting CPR done on him and all the lights still on him. A festival attendee walked up and stood there for a minute confused. He looked over to me "Is this a performance?"

I looked into his eyes. "No." What a strange scene it was to have all the stage lights shining on the Medics as they performed chest compressions and electric shocks. This went on for a long time, probably at least 20 minutes . After the sixth time they shocked him the machine said "Irregular pulse detected. No more shocks required."

The Medics stopped doing compressions and waited. It was very quiet and everybody watched. One of the doctors took his pulse, "He's got a pulse but its not very strong".

About five minutes later Jacques let out a gasp and a yell. We were all very surprised because for the last 15 minutes he was dead. He moaned some more and took some breaths and I was astounded that he had come back to life. The Medics did what they could to make him comfortable. They had broken his ribs in the CPR process so he was in pain, but he was conscious. The ambulance arrived with lights flashing as people walked by entering the festival. They put him in the ambulance and drove him to the field near us where a rescue helicopter landed and took Jacques to St Josephs in Bellingham 35 miles away.

As it departed it flew right over the event as everyone partied below. I am so thankful that we had a great team of Medics and nurses on hand as well as an AED defibrillator. Without this Jacques would certainly be dead now. The next day I heard he was going into surgery and I was still in awe of what had happened. Jacques had died onstage and was brought back to life. Had he died it would have been a very different outcome and possibly have been the end of the Imagine Festival. Very thankful he is still with us to share his story as he has a lot of knowledge to share about the unfolding of psychedelic culture".

The following passage was written by Tracia the trauma nurse who brought me back and illustrates the powerful impact this type of event can have on all involved.

Tracia said, "Such a pivotal moment for me Friday 13 under a full moon at Imagine festival of all things just after eleven pm. Jacques and I stepped into each other's heart spaces in the Revival Tent stage, under a huge white heart. Forever we are both changed. He does not know how profoundly he has impacted my life.

I had created an identity for myself. I resonated with this identity strongly, and it was an integral part of how I knew myself; a coping skill I learned, as a very young child strengthened by relationships and situations that perpetuated this false self-identity. It served me quite well for most of my life.

After finding you Jacques, my lizard brain took over, not thinking, just responding and time slowed. There was one split second where I surveyed the scene and looked into the eyes of someone I knew, my friend Danielle who was standing close by watching. It shook me for a moment. I saw that she was intensely watching, then my lizard brain took over and your heart had all of my focus.

After you were safely transported I was surrounded by people wanting to thank me and offer genuine gratitude for my actions. I was truly horrified. I could not get away from the attention. I realized I had gone into action on stage in front of an audience of your friends, my friends and my lover. I felt exposed, vulnerable and completely outside of my comfort zone. This realization began to sink in, like really sink in.

As that full moon waned and began to get bright again, so did my cycle of grief. A little leak began in my heart that night and I cried every day for a month. My whole being was out of sorts, my head fuzzy, my feet unsteady. I could not understand why I was feeling so completely shaken, my emotions raw, tired yet unable to sleep. Each time you reached out to me, anxiety took hold and I did not understand why. You traveled to see me, to thank me, my heart felt your genuine love and gratitude. I do not have the words to tell you how that moment touched me. It was felt purely by spirit and words do not exist to express my heart. Jacques, whereas my spirit refused to give up on your heart that night you refused to allow me to dismiss myself, to shy away from genuine appreciation. You do not even know the gift you have given me.

This old identity, she was not going away easily, but she is not who I am any longer. I spent two nights camping under the next full moon, healing at the Land. This is where the leak in my heart healed.

I literally woke up Tuesday after Sunday's full moon with clarity and compassion for myself and gave myself a big hug and told myself how much I love *me*! It may be the first time in my life I've said these words to myself.

After several days of admiring the box you sent me I finally opened your gift. It is phenomenal, *I love it soooo much*.

Thank you, Jacques my life is forever irrevocably changed since we met Friday September 13, 2019 under the Harvest Full Moon." Tracia Libentia

I sent her a work of art in the shape of a heart made from pieces of metal welded together by my friend Doug.

In a later conversation in early 2020 with Tracia she told me that at around six on the night of Friday the 13th she had participated in a group Cacao ceremony in the Revival tent on the same stage where five hours later she saved my life. She said that at one point in the ceremony she had an ineffable transcendent experience of the web of Universal Oneness where none of us is separate from the other, where all life forms are interdependent on each other. Without Tracia being alive and present at my moment of death I would not be alive now, proving her point. This might also explain my extreme love of chocolate!

Given the razor thin odds of my survival on September 13, 2019 and the perfect set of preconditions in place for what happened, I can only say that I experienced Divine Intervention or Perfect Alignment to Source or the Grace of God, Goddess, Gaia. Divine Intervention and Amazing Good Fortune, something impossible to have been predicted. I had imagined and designed my life to end and be reborn at that moment in time. A lifetime of surrendering to my heart had led me to this perfect moment where the loving actions of humans saved me, giving me more moments to finish this book and music. Everyone and everything played a crucial part for the outcome to be as it is right now and I am grateful beyond words.

Me   Mel Seme

Tracia   Me

HEART OF THE MATTER

My life has been a continuous rehearsal for death in the form of psychedelic journeys that allowed me to let go of old patterns and be reborn into new levels of awareness, sensitivity, and refinement.

Les petite mortes.

The heart is the center of our being, the engine of life that feeds our body with blood and all of the nutrients that keep us alive. It is central to our consciousness and when it is strong and in rhythm so too are we. It is the universal symbol of love and emotion and the organ that keeps us in motion and animated. It is the Yin to the brains Yang in our physical manifestation.

Heart dis-ease is the number one cause of death in our culture which is understandable given the level of stress and thing fetishes we are bombarded with. Take good care of your heart as if your life depends on it because it does.

Bless and protect all of our sacred hearts.

ICU DREAM

9.25.19 1:30am

I distinctly remember a dream I had while in ICU following my open heart surgery:

My body hovered about twenty feet over the surface of a hillside navigating toward an electrical radioactive vapor cloud that began pulsing and growing stronger, emitting a low hum.

I was certain this was it, and it was time to leave my body. As I approached the moment of merging with the vapor cloud I moved toward it. As it intensified I knew that it was time to settle down on the ground into its glow and lie down to surrender my human form and become one with Great Spirit. I started toning to match its frequency to become one with it in resonant essence energy so that I could dissolve and merge.

The process of letting go into a greater energy intensified when I tuned into its frequency like turning the knobs of an old radio and tuning into the Cosmic Radio Station. When I found the spot free of static I settled to earth toning louder to match the cloud's tone in anticipation of the moment the energies would merge and life would leave my body as a container for the energy that was me. Open Heart Music poured from my body, with the first word. OHM. As I settled it faded causing me to awaken from this final Dream of passing while OHM-ing. Once I realized it was a dream I awakened and called the nurse.

I later learned that while I was dreaming they almost lost me when my heart went back into AFIB but they were able to restore it to a normal sinus rhythm. I intuited that we all choose our specific exit point from this life and most probably our entrance point as well.

It took twelve days and nights in the ICU of St Joseph's Peace hospital to recover from major heart surgery before I was released. Countless pokes, prods, blood draws, and tubes confined and restricted my movement making activity impossible. By the tenth day my body became toxic due to my inability to have a bowel movement from lack of activity causing me to become highly agitated. Nurses refer to this as Pump Head which causes the patient to go temporarily crazy until they can eliminate with a bowel movement.

I started to think that they were trying to kill me and demanded to see my doctor. Angel nurses who have to deal with this often did their best to facilitate a bowel movement on my part to no avail. The opiates and drugs had constipated me. I demanded to be released from the hospital but was not ready to be released. Everyone did their best to explain it to me, but I was crazed and demanded to be released. After seeing my doctor and rejecting his position, they reluctantly removed the tubes in my stomach and all of the life support, allowing me to be discharged from St Josephs.

I called a cab to transport me thirty miles to Island Hospital in Anacortes at a cost of one hundred fifty dollars where they admitted me to the ER and left me alone for a couple of hours. After speaking to the head nurse and my son Max on the phone, I realized that I had been unreasonable and made a mistake. Max told me they wanted me back at St Josephs and would provide an ambulance for my return with no hard feelings.

I humbly returned with my tail between my legs and promised to follow everyone's instructions. That night I had four huge bowel movements that had been stimulated by all the walking I had done, so in the end my breakout was a positive thing, but embarrassing for me and annoying to the hospital staff.

Eternal gratitude goes to Dr. Douglas and the doctors and staff of St. Josephs Peace Hospital in Bellingham WA. for providing me with the best possible care. I honor and bless them all.

As a result of my imminent death I wrote my own obituary:

Eulogy for Poloka LeLe

In Loving memory of Jacques Olivier (aka Poloka Lele)
Hawaiian for Flying Frog
He Lived
He Loved
He played
He sang
He Danced
He Dreamed
He Laughed
He Cried
He Croaked
He gives Salutations to Supreme Consciousness
He Dances Alone
He has returned to Source
He is at Peace Now

POST SURGERY

I had a daily realization of enhanced cognitive and communicative abilities post death. Things that were previously problems were easily solved. Ideas flowed freely with no obstruction or interruption of energy or vision, manifestation, or completion as a result of being in the gamma state for an extended period. There is a Hawaiian word "Kala" meaning "there are no limits" which is how I was feeling, and I have become a   testament to the healing power and magical energy that Orcas Island holds.

Love is the glue that holds everything together. It is an act of love that creates us, and countless acts of love keep us alive and thriving. There is only Love or a crying out for love in every thought, word, and deed. Surrounding myself with love and radiating it from my soul with intention and action in my life is fulfilling in miraculous ways.

Many in their later years experience hanging on in a quiet desperation as they lose loved ones, fortunes, physical strength, mental capacities, social status, their minds, and eventually their life. The world seems to abandon them. I find it important to stay in service and connected to others. I've been to all of these places yet I would not trade places with anyone else that ever lived and died. I have a new life, a second chance, a reboot, and a rebirth that I cherish with every breath. I savor every moment and connect deeper with others because I know that life is a precious gift and opportunity to experience love and to be loved. I have seen the End, been granted an extension, and relate to Terence's final year of grace and gratitude from my direct experience. I'm still riding high on this rollercoaster called life which I know as fleeting and fragile. Savoring it and honoring all forms with respect and reverence is essential. Life is love is life. Or as my father was fond of saying, "Live and let live, love and let love."

I was not conscious of it at the time, but moving to Orcas Island began the orchestration of my own death. Losing three people closest to me created a mindset best described as a loss of purpose or a feeling of irrelevance. Like many others in their later years I accepted the notion that the real juice of my life might be gone and that the best was behind me. My life had been amazing and on some level I desired to join my loved ones in the infinite and be at peace, to essentially call it a life.

All is vibration and resonance. The frequency you emanate is what you attract and getting a second chance at life after sidestepping the Grin Reaper has eliminated my death wish. It will come soon enough, but it is nothing to fear or dwell on. Suffering is optional, but I had none. It's not over until its over and I have embraced life with renewed vigor and enthusiasm. This book is testament to that. We don't fully appreciate things until they are gone and my good fortune on Friday the thirteenth is driven home by the realization that if the same event occurred now, my chances of survival would be close to zero. The likelihood of being close to someone capable of CPR and having shock paddles, even when surrounded by millions of people is highly unlikely.

As of September 13, 2020 on the one year anniversary of the event I am working on this book. Due to the Covid 19 pandemic the world has changed exposing shadow and forcing many to confront their own demise. I was found on social media after thirty-five years by Colette, a magical woman whom I had met in 1985 in an after hours LA club called Zero which was frequented by musicians and performers after a gig with the Mutts. I was 29 and at the peak of my physical attractiveness and musical abilities when our eyes met, though brief, our connection felt profoundly intense and powerfully magnetic. It is strange to think of the possibility of having crossed over in 2019 and missing reconnection with her. This also applies to my cousin Carole, my first big crush. I reconnected with her on social media in August 2020 after 41 years. What a gift and blessing it is to still be here and witness and welcome the birth of my first grandson, Cairo Wolfe Olivier on November 21, 2020. I video chatted with him on his second day on earth and was overwhelmed with optimism and love while realizing how different the world he will inherit is from anything in the past.

My death at Imagine changed my story and allowed me to re-define myself. Since 2011 I had been living a story of grief and loss, a sad and depressing one that defined who I was.

My new story is one of redemption, renewal, and the shift in my energy has attracted beautiful events and blessings into my life, including this book. After this experience I feel that my life, and legacy consists of the following:

1. My genetic blueprint, descendents or children.

2. My Art, and contributions to humanity.

3. Whose hearts I have touched or how I made people feel when in my presence, how others experienced my energy, how I loved and was loved, and the depth of my integrity.

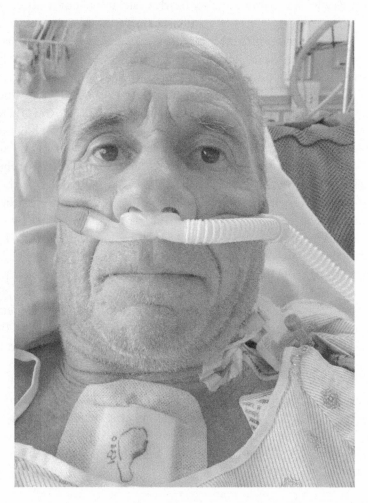

SWEET SURRENDER

As Terence McKenna elegantly stated about the miracle of the body that we take for granted: "There will be a real Shamanism, a new shamanism, one practiced in the full light of science and in the full light of a global data processing capacity."

His observation that all systems and processes are similar across scale and that reality is fractal is profound. He was a true visionary as we watch the story of humans unfold.

Indigenous people preserve the spirit and natural ways of being in the world and we have explored a technological path of material expression and a hybrid style of Spirit and Matter.

The Union of Spirit and Matter is all inclusive. This is love and love is the key to salvation.

Love Wins.

In my recovery I have experienced real and specific interactions between dream states, waking states, sub consciousness, and conscious sensory perceptions. The death experience represents a full integration of all of these states coming together to create the reality that occurred for me at a special moment in time, the dissolution of boundaries, and harmonizing with the Infinite. The Gamma state is entered when the body shuts down. Brain activity continues and increases in an attempt to revive the body, so even without a heartbeat the brain is active directing all of its capacity to the act of survival.

Out of all the drugs I have sampled and worked with 5MEO DMT comes closest to this state of consciousness.

"Row row row your boat gently down the stream,
merrily merrily merrily life is but a dream".... ???

"Posthumous glory is where the action is."
Terence McKenna 1999

Is this laughing
Or am I crying
There is no living without dying
As old self sheds away
So that I may live another day
To stare death's horror in the face
And re-emerge so full of grace

Poloka LeLe 2020

REFLECTIONS

Another aspect of this event is that I was able to see the events that took place after I died. The chain of communication that the news traveled through and the people I was connected to fascinated me. I had imagined in previous near death experiences what might happen in the aftermath, but this time it really happened. The removal of my self gives me perspective on the transient nature of existence. Humanity is in the throes of growing pains that come with new possibilities, new dimensions, new realities, and relationships to life and death. The possibility of transcending physical death by merging with machines and artificial intelligence loom on the horizon, but nothing lasts forever.

Whatever else it may be, life is an extraordinary opportunity to live with passion with the heart being the core inspiration. Surrendering to death is an act of Love. Life is short, precious, and magical, not to be taken too personally. It's just a ride. Life can be seen as an amusement park full of rides as varied and unique as there are humans and all other conscious beings for that matter. We are the designers, builders, owner operators, and best customers for our own rides here on Magic Mushroom Mountain. Take full responsibility, relax and enjoy the ride.

Mind is primary to human experience. Emotion expressed through art is what separates man from machine, and attachment is our constant adversary, forcing us into feeling our deepest emotions. Soul is the energetic signature of being and love. Humor is essential to our nature, reminding us to not take the ride personally. Live with light-heartedness. The Cosmic Joke is on *all* of us. No one gets out alive.

Psychedelics can reduce fear and desire, bringing peace of mind, allowing us to live in paradise. The primary value of psychedelics is to quell the anxieties brought on by ego in all its complexity and to give us the simple perspective and powers of self reflection to embrace and love our transition from physical to spiritual realms.

"I stopped by Satan's house
Regret is in the kitchen making coffee
The three daughters of Satan
Desire, Fulfillment, Regret"

Author unknown

"Desire is the cause of all suffering".   Buddah

POWER OF ART

The psychedelic community has been a conundrum to our culture mostly mediated through art. Terence McKenna once said "Don't be shy. It is our duty as Artists to convey the psychedelic message.

Put the art pedal to the metal".

That was in 1999, twenty-one years ago which was the spirit of the time. Some of us took his advice. Now with the legalization of cannabis along with growing awareness of plant medicines like Ayahuasca, psilocybin, and the decriminalization in cities across the US, psychedelics have been granted greater legal status in therapeutic settings integrating them into the larger collective consciousness. In the last twenty years I have witnessed countless breakthroughs and transformations in peoples lives and have become a cheerleader for consciousness expansion and expression through music and books like this one. The highs of being in love and fulfillment, the lows of loss and disappointment. The exhilaration of being on a rollercoaster or another thrilling ride in the amusement park of life is the point and end in and of itself. To feel it and honor it with all of our heart and to have Courage to let the mystery of life have its way in spite of resistance that creates counter resistance.

Surrender is the opposite of giving up by harmonizing with environment rather than fighting it. Soft always wins. You have got to let the strange hands touch you. Navigate toward the beautiful because what is good and what is true is slippery. These are some of the takeaways from those years spent with Terence and has been my strategy for the incredible outcomes described in this story. We have seen a shift to a technologically dominant landscape where computers are in charge, just as Terence foreshadowed in 1999. AI is here whether we like it or not and we are in a profound adjustment period of growing pains as the caterpillar morphs into a butterfly. Humor and courage are our medicines in my humble opinion.

"Lighten Up"
Terence McKenna

"If wishes were horses, beggars would ride.
Mind wraps back looking at itself.
As one dimension fills up, its spills over into the next.
The process is hungry for complexity, and is a novelty producing engine. What are the limits to artificial intelligence?
If there are no limits, then psychedelics are key".
Terence McKenna 1999

UNION OF OPPOSITES

The paradox of existence is that everything implies its opposite.

There is always a polarity in things that span the spectrum of reality, and all experience is ultimately one. This is why the pain of separation and loss actually feel good. In the same way that we are all unique with specific preferences and personalities, we all have the same needs, desires and characteristics at different points of awareness in the full spectrum of reality. Our diversity and uniqueness of experience is what makes life interesting at times causing conflict and disagreement. Goodwill is essential. The point of living is acceptance and surrender.

It is important that we tolerate and champion each other's differences which is the celebration of our differences that brings harmony and love into the world. Terence recognized this in his theory of novelty stating that all events break down into habit, novelty, repetition, change, tension and release. All of it is valid within the experience. Terence's idea that the process is a novelty producing engine speaks to the endless combination of things that are possible and occurring in evolution. The singularity represents the moment when all that can occur has occurred and exists at the end of time. Where we all come from and where we all return to. The eternal light of loving awareness. When all is love and love is all. This is where we are headed and why we are all here. To be part of the celebration and dance of life, to enjoy the ride and be fully awake in our collective dream. To be of service and to feel deeply without prejudice or expectation is the nectar of life. Be kind to one another because it is yourself to whom you are being kind to.

THE LIGHT AND THE DARK

There is a union of opposites and a middle way with many shades of gray connecting the extremes of black and white. A natural progression emerges when people experiment with psychedelics. If careful attention is paid to set and setting, the first few experiences can be ecstatic as the tripper has the veils lifted and sees the world in a refreshing new light. They get a free pass from spirit to dance in the fields of joy and laughter without restriction or inhibition. Their lives are enhanced and transformed for the better and they are open to continue their personal exploration on the path of expanded consciousness. If set and setting are ignored the experience can spiral downward into a "bad trip" usually resulting in an end of experimentation by the tripper.

According to Jung, we all develop a shadow self that is kept hidden for the most part from the world at large. This is where the ego forms a defense to the world and differentiation occurs. Us and them. Everyone enters the world with trauma, leaving the safety and comfort of mothers womb to be exposed to the world and needing to survive on their own by breathing and eating independent from the safety of mother's body. Everyone has something happen in their life that is Traumatic. When someone has a "bad trip" it is the shadow being is exposed.

The ability of psychedelics to suppress the ego may be the most valuable aspect of the healing properties they possess. Boundary dissolution and the sense of timelessness combine to connect us to the greater whole of everything that ever was, is, and will be. A healthy ego is necessary to create healthy boundaries between people and the world, but it cannot be allowed to run the show. When it does it can manifest in narcissism and lack of empathy, a problem we face as a species today.

Difficult trips are often the most therapeutic in confronting and dealing with trauma, A purge, or letting go of outdated beliefs and habits to reboot of our neural operating system, just what the doctor or shaman ordered in the process of healing. Near death experiences produce an altered state of consciousness similar to some psychedelic states which are valuable as a bridge between life and death by reducing fear and anxiety surrounding the end of life, reassuring us that we are more than our bodies. Each of us represents a single point of awareness essential to the entire lifeForce of the Universe. It is the charge and responsibility of each of us to optimize our individual selves in the interest of the whole of Life. We all know this in our deepest heart of hearts, yet can be distracted and forget this basic truth. Love connects and inspires us to be our best and highest self to be all we can be.

Nothing is insignificant and everything matters on a micro and macro level. There is nothing to do but the act of being and bearing witness with awareness. Enjoy the ride, its ups, downs, twists turns, stops, and starts, all necessary and essential elements of life experience, the key being surrender which requires courage and trust.

From "***Death, A Love Story***" by ***Matthew J. Pallamary***

Death speaking :

"Yes I am coming for you or you're coming for me. It's all a matter of perspective. I could come at any moment no matter how old or how young you are. I can take you in a heartbeat, a breath, a flash, or I can take you slowly on the installment plan. I can even take you before you ever get into the world. I can be gentle and slip you away in the darkest depths of unconsciousness where you never know what happened, or I can sneak up on you mid-dream, maybe as a character, a friend or loved one and welcome you home that way. The variations are Endless, I have many names and faces in a multitude of times and places so your choices are only limited by your imagination. If any of my many faces and facets do come to you, then your expectation took part in the creation of that moment, making you the co-creator of that Moment.

It is the Great Mystery where we are from and where we are going, and part of the fun is that ***Anything Can Happen***. You could even come home to me with an Open Heart the way I receive you without any judgements or expectations."

The final, most amazing irony in this story full of synchronicities is Mateo's recent book, ***Death: (A Love Story)*** was completed in July 2019.

I died in September 2019.

We were both unaware of what the other was doing during this time. In an expanding wave of ironies, ***Death: (A Love Story)*** was officially released on January 6, 2020, in conjunction with the onset of the covid pandemic, and as fate would have it, the infamous Trump inspired storming of the U.S. Capitol occurred on this exact same date one year later in 2021.

ABSOLUTE PEACE NOW

There are moments of perfect alignment in life where tears of sorrow become tears of joy in an exquisite dance where emotion becomes an all encompassing feeling of connection and gratitude. At those moments we are aligned with the nature of the mysterious miracle that is life where we realize that all is connected, where the Quantum field, the Matrix, God, or whatever you choose to call it is fully exposed and we are vulnerable and fully engaged in Oneness.

Absolute unconditional love for self allows us to love everyone and everything else in our lives. It is in these moments when we are fully in tune and engaged with the universe by transcending the indifference and illusion of separateness that our egos perpetuate.

These moments are mercurial and the Source of all art and all that is beautiful and true. These moments only come in times of grace and surrender to the energies that swirl around and through us. It is this that I will miss the most when I take my final breath and become spirit, when life leaves my body and merges with the infinite. I have been fortunate to experience this many times and recognize the beauty of all beings and things that inhabit existence. May you be equally blessed as you create and navigate your own personal ride on the merry go round of Life.

EPILOGUE

I am more aware of the full circle nature of Being as I continue living into the twenty-first century.

My past year of extended life has seen many circles of completion, not the least of which has been the birth of my Cairo Wolfe Olivier in November 21, 2020. Had I died at Imagine I would have missed this experience along with what is yet to come.

The story of my life continues to unfold in miraculous ways. I wrote much of the last few chapters in a coffee shop in Encinitas, California called Surf Dog owned by Dave, the former manager of English Beat, an eighties band whose big hit was Red Red Wine. I remember seeing Tim Leary with Laura in Encinitas in 1978 at La Paloma theater when he was performing his stand up philosophy tour after Governor Jerry Brown commuted his prison sentence. I was inspired by him at the age of twenty-four.

When my fiancé Jacqueline was fighting for her life in 2010 and I was driving south to sell my RV, Surf Dog cafe was my destination. I was going to meet someone name Dave. Ten years later and I am writing my memoir.

I have a new Grandson and I have just moved into a new apartment on Orcas and traded up my vehicle to a 2000 Toyota Sienna from a 1978 Toyota Chinook. Here on Orcas I am finishing this story with a happy ending and new beginning.

Everyone has a story and this has been mine. Now I am looking forward to making the third act in the Play of Life a great one now that I have been granted the opportunity to keep writing and making more music because Nature Loves Courage.

Peace and Aloha

"The Center Of The Universe Is Right Between Yours Eyes But Home Is Where The Heart Is"   Matthew J. Pallamary

"THE UNIVERSE PREFERS JOY"   T McKenna

DEDICATION

I dedicate his book to Monique and George my parents who brought me into this world, to Tracia Libentia , the nurse who brought me back to life who refused to let me die with her loving determination, and to all of the other people who had a hand in my survival and to Mel Seme who caught me as I fell, preventing further damage to my head, to Darin Leong for giving me the opportunity to share my music at that particular moment at IMAGINE festival, and to Dr Douglas the surgeon who rebuilt my heart and the other doctors, nurses, and staff at St. Joseph's Peace Hospital in Bellingham Washington for their excellent care and attention, and of course to the EMT and ambulance staff who kept me alive and got me to the hospital.

I also wish to acknowledge Terence McKenna for his inspiration and guidance in my pursuit of expanded consciousness through the plant spirits, and **Matthew J. (MATEO) Pallamary**, my friend, fellow psychonaut, editor, and writing guru for his patience, undying guidance, and humor, and to my son Max for being born and making me a better man for it, to Hoku for being my unconditionally loving partner through it all, and finally to Laura, Jacqueline, Ashley, Dakini, the women who love me. Gracias por todo.

http://www.icaropublishing.com/

Cairo Wolfe Olivier

Terence McKenna – Art by Jin An Wong

Made in the USA
Monee, IL
14 October 2021